BY THE EDITORS OF CONSUMER GUIDE®

FAVORITE
Italian
BRAND NAME RECIPES

BEEKMAN HOUSE
New York

Contents

Louis Weber, President
Publications International, Ltd.
3841 West Oakton Street
Skokie, IL 60076

Permission is never granted for commercial purposes.

This edition published by:
Beekman House
Distributed by Crown Publishers, Inc.

Cover Design: Linda Snow Shum

ISBN 0-517-60407-8

Printed and bound by Pomurski tisk, Yugoslavia

h g f e d c

COVER RECIPES
Front Cover:
Left: ''Antipasto Salad''
    Campbell Soup Co.
Right: ''Beans and Spaghetti Carbonara''
    General Foods
Back Cover:
Left: ''Shortcut Pizzas''
    Hunt-Wesson Kitchens
Right: ''Saronno Panettone''
    Foreign Vintages, Inc.

Introduction

A collection of Italian recipes to suit every taste! *Your* favorites—the best loved, most collected recipes from food companies and manufacturers, combined into this one taste-tempting cookbook. These are the recipes you wished you had cut out from boxtops, side panels and labels of food packages or from newspaper and magazine advertisements.

Recipes for hundreds of Italian favorites, from everyone's favorite spaghetti and pizza to specialties like elegant panettone, luscious linguine, hearty minestrone soup, spicy cacciatore—and more. If spaghetti is your dish, take a look at some of our choices: Meatless Spaghetti, Garden Spaghetti, Sausage Spaghetti, and of course, Spaghetti with Meat Sauce. Surely a recipe to please everyone!

You can create a super delicious Italian meal with this collection of appetizers, soups, salads, pastas, desserts and more!

An easy-to-use INDEX is provided so that you can locate a recipe by its title, by the brand name product used in the recipe, or by the main food ingredient, such as ''chicken.''

For your convenience, an address directory of all food manufacturers listed in the book has also been included (see ACKNOWLEDGMENTS). The recipes in this book are reprinted exactly as they appear on the food packages or in the advertisements. Any questions or comments regarding the recipes should be directed to the individual manufacturers for prompt attention. All of the recipes have been copyrighted by the food manufacturers and cannot be reprinted without their permission. By printing these recipes, CONSUMER GUIDE® is *not* endorsing particular brand name foods.

Appetizers

Antipasto

1 head **California ICEBERG Lettuce**
½ cup olive or salad oil
¼ cup wine vinegar
2 tablespoons grated onion
2 cloves garlic, crushed
1 teaspoon salt
½ teaspoon freshly ground black pepper
1 can (1 pound) garbanzo beans, or chick peas
1 can (6 ounces) mushroom caps, drained
2 jars (6 ounces *each*) marinated artichoke hearts
¼ pound sliced salami
1 can (4 ounces) peperoncini, or green chili peppers

Core, rinse and thoroughly drain lettuce; refrigerate in plastic bag or plastic crisper. Combine oil, vinegar, onion, garlic, salt and pepper. Divide this marinade in half. Toss garbanzo beans with half of dressing. Toss mushrooms with remaining dressing. Chill at least one hour. Separate lettuce into 5 cups and arrange on platter. Heap beans, mushrooms, artichoke hearts, salami and peperoncini into lettuce cups. *Makes 6 servings*

Favorite recipe from **California Iceberg Lettuce Commission**

Creamy Cucumber Antipasto

1 container (8 ounces) plain low-fat yogurt
2 tablespoons distilled white vinegar
2 tablespoons chopped fresh chives
2 teaspoons dillweed
1 teaspoon celery seed
2 packets **SWEET 'N LOW®**
½ teaspoon salt
½ teaspoon dry mustard
Dash freshly ground pepper
3 medium-size cucumbers, peeled and sliced thin

In a bowl, combine all ingredients except cucumbers. Mix thoroughly. Toss cucumber slices in dressing and marinate several hours in refrigerator. *8 servings*

PER SERVING (½ cup): Calories: 25   Protein: 2gm
Carbohydrate: 5gm   Fat: trace   Sodium: 160mg

snack mate.

Snack Mate Antipasto

1 (20-ounce) can chick peas, drained
2 (14-ounce) cans artichoke hearts, drained
1 cup Italian-style bottled salad dressing
6 hard-cooked eggs for Cheese Topped Deviled Eggs*
1 (4⅝-ounce) can **SNACK MATE Pasteurized Process Cheese Spread**, any flavor
12 cherry tomatoes, tops removed
6 stalks celery, cut into 2-inch lengths
¼ pound thinly sliced salami, rolled into cone shapes and secured with wooden toothpicks
Lettuce leaves
2 small zucchini, thinly sliced on diagonal (about 2 cups)
Pimiento-stuffed olives

1. In 1½-quart shallow glass baking dish, combine drained chick peas and artichoke hearts; toss with salad dressing to coat well. Cover and marinate in refrigerator 4 hours or overnight.
2. Prepare Cheese Topped Deviled Eggs*. Use **SNACK MATE Cheese** to top tomatoes and fill celery stalks and salami cones.
3. Line individual salad plates or large platter with lettuce leaves. Using slotted spoon, drain chick peas and artichoke hearts from marinade; arrange on plates or platter with deviled eggs, tomatoes, celery, salami, zucchini and olives. *Makes 12 servings*

*Cheese Topped Deviled Eggs

Cut 6 hard-cooked eggs in half lengthwise; remove yolks and place in small bowl. Mash yolks with fork, adding 2 tablespoons mayonnaise, 1 tablespoon each chopped parsley, chopped onion and Dijon-style mustard and ¼ teaspoon liquid hot pepper seasoning. Spoon into egg white halves and top each with **SNACK MATE Cheese**. *Makes 12 Deviled Eggs*

Antipasto Pizza Appetizer

Crust:
½ cup soy oil margarine, softened
½ cup Cheddar cheese spread, softened
1¼ cups flour
1 teaspoon Italian seasoning herbs

Preheat oven to 350°F. In a food processor mix flour, margarine, cheese spread, and herbs just until blended. Pat into a greased 12-inch pizza pan. Bake 12 to 15 minutes or until lightly browned. Cool thoroughly.

Filling:
¼ cup soy oil mayonnaise
1 (8 oz.) package cream cheese, softened
1 (4.2 oz.) can chopped black olives
¼ cup chopped pimento stuffed green olives

Suggested toppings:
Thinly sliced salami, chopped tomatoes, sliced green onions, chopped green pepper, sliced mushrooms

Cream together cream cheese and mayonnaise. Fold in olives. Spread mixture on cooled crust. Arrange the suggested toppings over filling. Refrigerate. Cut into thin wedges and serve with a fork. To serve as a finger food, cut an additional circle three inches from outer rim.   *Makes 16 to 32 servings*

Favorite recipe from **American Soybean Association**

Spinach-Stuffed Mushrooms

1½ cups cooked, chopped spinach
12 extra-large (2½ inch) mushroom caps*
¾ cup **NALLEY®'S Mayonnaise**
¼ cup grated Parmesan cheese
¼ cup fine dry bread crumbs
2 Tbsp. sherry
2 tsp. lemon juice
½ tsp. salt

Drain spinach, pressing out liquid. Wash mushrooms; remove and chop stems, reserving caps. Mix mayonnaise with remaining ingredients. Stir in spinach and chopped stems. Heap mixture into caps. Arrange in oiled pans and bake in 350° oven 15 to 20 minutes.   *Makes 6 servings*

*For hors d'oeuvre, use small mushrooms.

Savory Stuffed Mushrooms

24 medium mushrooms
⅓ cup seeded and finely chopped tomato
¼ cup finely chopped green pepper
2 tablespoons sliced scallions
⅓ cup low-calorie Italian dressing
SNACK MATE Chive 'n Onion or **Cheese 'n Bacon Pasteurized Process Cheese Spread**

1. Remove stems from mushroom caps; chop stems and blend with tomato, green pepper and scallions. Place mushroom caps and vegetable mixture in baking dish.
2. Pour dressing over mushroom caps and vegetable mixture. Cover and refrigerate at least 4 hours or overnight, turning mushroom caps occasionally. Drain caps on paper towels before stuffing.
3. Spoon vegetable mixture evenly into mushroom caps. Garnish with **SNACK MATE Cheese**.   *Makes 24 mushrooms*

Sizzlean® Stuffed Mushrooms Florentine

7 strips **SIZZLEAN®**
24 medium-sized fresh mushrooms
2 tablespoons butter or margarine
2 tablespoons finely chopped onion
5 ounces frozen chopped spinach, thawed and squeezed dry
½ cup grated Swiss cheese
1 egg, beaten
¼ teaspoon ground nutmeg
¼ teaspoon salt
2 tablespoons dry bread crumbs
Grated Parmesan cheese

Cook **SIZZLEAN®** according to package directions. Drain and chop finely.

Wash mushrooms; snap out stems and chop fine. Cook in butter with onion until lightly browned. Remove from heat. Add chopped **SIZZLEAN®** and remaining ingredients (except Parmesan cheese) and mix well.

Fill mushroom caps with mixture. Sprinkle with Parmesan cheese. Bake in 350°F oven for 20 minutes. Serve hot.
                    Yield: 24 appetizers

Pizza Roll® Pasta Snack Dip Tray

Pour 1 cup spaghetti or pizza sauce into 8-inch cake pan. Top with 1 cup finely shredded mozzarella cheese. Surround with 12 to 24 **JENO'S® PIZZA ROLLS® Pasta Snacks** on a baking sheet. Bake at 375° F for fifteen minutes.   *Serves 4 to 6*

Armanino's Pesto Pizza

Pizza dough
8 oz. sliced black olives
2½ lb. shredded mozzarella cheese
12 oz. grated Parmesan cheese
1 oz. **ARMANINO FARMS Freeze-dried Mushrooms**
1 oz. **ARMANINO FARMS Freeze-dried Scallions**
1½ quarts **ARMANINO FARMS Frozen** or **Prepared Freeze-dried Pesto**

Roll dough, cut into 50 2-inch rounds. Place freeze-dried scallions in colander, run hot water through to rehydrate. Place freeze-dried mushrooms in colander, run hot water through to rehydrate. Spread each dough round generously with Pesto mix, portion other ingredients as topping on each with grated cheese added last. Bake at 350° approximately 10 minutes, until lightly browned.

50 2-inch cocktail portions

Fried Mozzarella
(Fritto di Mozzarella)

1 pound mozzarella cheese
2 tablespoons flour
2 eggs, slightly beaten
About ¾ cup dry bread crumbs
1 can (8 oz.) tomato sauce
¼ cup sliced pimiento-stuffed **DURKEE Spanish Olives**
½ teaspoon **DURKEE Sweet Basil**
Vegetable oil

Cut cheese in ½-inch slices, then in fingers or wedges. Coat with flour; dip in eggs, then in bread crumbs. Place on plate lined with waxed paper, cover and chill at least one hour. In small sauce pan heat tomato sauce, olives and basil; keep warm. Fry cheese in 2 inches of hot oil (380°) until pale yellow. Drain on paper towels. Serve at once with tomato-olive sauce.

Makes about 20 fingers, 10 appetizer or 4 luncheon servings

VARIATIONS:
Add **DURKEE Salad Herbs** to bread crumbs before coating cheese. Dip fried cheese in **DURKEE Famous Sauce**.

Peperoni Whip

5 ounce package **SWIFT PREMIUM® PEPERONI®**
2 packages (3 ounces each) cream cheese
½ cup whipping cream, whipped
4 tablespoons chopped parsley

BLENDER METHOD:
Hold peperoni under running hot water and remove skin. Slice into ¼ inch slices; then in half. Grind on "low" or "chop" speed. Add cream cheese, whipped cream and parsley. Blend until just mixed; stopping blender to scrape down sides if necessary. Serve with crackers, Melba toast or toasted party rye bread.

FOOD PROCESSOR METHOD:
Cut skinned peperoni into small chunks. Using cutting blade, chop peperoni and remove from bowl. Chop parsley and remove. Cut cream cheese into cubes and process until smooth. Add peperoni and parsley to cheese. Process to mix. Remove from bowl and combine with whipping cream.

Yield: 2 cups

Pasta Snacks

Assorted pasta (such as bow ties, wheels, and spirals)
CRISCO® Shortening for deep frying
Seasoned salt

In a large saucepan, cook the pasta in boiling salted water till tender, yet firm, about 10 minutes. If desired, keep the various shapes of pasta separate while cooking and frying. Drain the pasta very thoroughly. Fry pasta, a few pieces at a time, in deep **CRISCO®** heated to 365°. Fry till pasta is golden, about 2 minutes. Drain on paper toweling. Immediately sprinkle generously with seasoned salt. Serve warm or cool.

Italian Meat Balls on Picks

1 lb. ground beef
1 cup (4 oz.) shredded **STELLA Provolone Cheese**
2 teaspoons garlic salt
1½ teaspoons Italian seasoning
½ cup bread crumbs
1 egg, slightly beaten
½ cup tomato sauce

Combine all ingredients. Shape into 1-inch balls. Bake in shallow pan at 350° for 12 to 15 minutes. Serve on cocktail picks. These may be baked ahead of time and reheated just before serving.

60 to 70 meatballs

Dorman's®
Muenster-Anchovy Crisps

2 slices **DORMAN'S® Muenster Cheese**
⅓ cup flour
5 flat anchovy filets
Vegetable oil for deep-frying

In the top of a double boiler, over hot water, melt cheese. Add flour; stir with a fork until mixture forms a ball of dough. Turn out onto a very lightly floured board. Knead until well blended. Roll dough into a 10 x 4-inch rectangle. Arrange anchovies about 1-inch apart along the length of the dough. Fold over remaining dough, enclosing anchovies. Cut between anchovies, forming 5 strips. Heat oil to 360°. Deep fry until crisp and lightly browned. Drain on absorbent toweling.

Makes 5 crisps

DANNON® YOGURT
Yogurt Anchovy Egg Spread

6 hard boiled eggs, chopped
2 cups **DANNON® Plain Yogurt**
2 Tbsp. anchovy paste
¼ cup chopped scallions
12 olives, chopped
1 small dill pickle, chopped
Pepper to taste

In a bowl, mix eggs, yogurt, anchovy paste and scallions, olives and pickles. Season with pepper. Chill until ready to serve. Garnish with chopped chives. Serve spread on brown bread or crackers.

Marinated Oysters

1 pint oysters, fresh or frozen
2 cups cherry tomatoes
1½ cups fresh, whole mushrooms
6 green onions, cut into 2-inch lengths
¼ cup chopped pimiento
1 cup cider vinegar
½ cup salad or olive oil
½ cup water
2 cloves garlic, minced
1 teaspoon sugar
1 teaspoon salt
½ teaspoon dried oregano leaves, crumbled
¼ teaspoon pepper
Salad greens

Thaw oysters if frozen. Drain. Remove any remaining shell particles. Rinse tomatoes in cold water. Clean mushrooms thoroughly with a damp cloth. Cut large mushrooms in half. In a 2-quart bowl, combine oysters, tomatoes, mushrooms, green onions and pimiento. In a 1-quart bowl, combine remaining ingredients except salad greens; stir until sugar is dissolved. Pour marinade over oysters and vegetables. Cover loosely and marinate in the refrigerator at least 12 hours. Drain. Serve on salad greens.

Makes 6 servings, approximately 1½ quarts

Favorite recipe from **Gulf and South Atlantic Fisheries Development Foundation, Inc.**

Bertolli® Marinated Shrimp

1½ pounds cooked shrimp in shells
½ cup **BERTOLLI® Olive Oil**
¼ cup **BERTOLLI® Red Wine Vinegar**
2 tablespoons **BERTOLLI® Spaghetti Sauce**
2 tablespoons horseradish mustard
½ cup celery, minced
½ cup green onions, minced
½ cup drained capers
1 clove garlic, minced
1½ teaspoons paprika
½ teaspoon salt
Dash cayenne pepper
Shredded lettuce
Lemon wedges

Peel shrimp, leaving tails on. Mix remaining ingredients, except lettuce and lemon in medium bowl; stir in shrimp. Refrigerate covered 12 hours, stirring 2 or 3 times. Spoon onto lettuce-lined plate; garnish with lemon. *Makes 6-8 servings*

Icy Tomato Appetizer

1 can (16 ounce) **REDPACK Tomato Puree**
2 tablespoons chopped green onion
1 tablespoon lemon juice
½ cup water
2 teaspoons sugar
¾ teaspoon salt
½ teaspoon basil
1 stalk celery, finely chopped
2 drops hot pepper sauce
2 tablespoons minced parsley
1 can (7 ounce) shrimp, optional

In saucepan over medium-high heat, combine all ingredients except parsley and shrimp. Bring to boil; reduce heat to low, cover and simmer about 5 minutes. Pour into 8-inch square pan and stir in parsley. Place in freezer until mushy. Turn into mixing bowl and beat for about 4 minutes. Return to freezer until 15 minutes before serving time. Stir in shrimp and spoon into serving dishes. Garnish with shrimp, parsley sprig.

Serves 4 to 6

Eggplant
(Caponata)

1 med. eggplant
6 Tbsp. **FILIPPO BERIO Olive Oil**
1 sliced onion
3 Tbsp. tomato sauce
2 stalks celery diced
2 Tbsp. **FILIPPO BERIO Wine Vinegar**
1 Tbsp. sugar
1 Tbsp. capers
4 green olives stuffed with red peppers
¼ tsp. salt and ⅛ tsp. pepper

Peel eggplant and dice and fry in 5 Tbsp. **FILIPPO BERIO Olive Oil.** Remove eggplant from pan, add 1 additional Tbsp. of olive oil. Fry onions until brown. Add tomato sauce and celery— cook until celery is tender. If needed, add Tbsp. of water. Put back into pan cooked eggplant, capers and chopped olives. Heat Wine Vinegar with sugar and pour over eggplant. Salt and pepper to taste. Simmer for 10/15 minutes, stirring frequently. Serve cool in toasted squares of bread. Leftover can be put into refrigerator for later use.

100% PURE
Minute Maid®

Zippy Lemon Marinated Vegetable Hors d'Oeuvres

1 small cauliflower, broken into flowerets
2 green peppers, cut into ½-inch strips
½ pound small mushroom caps
5¼ ounce can black pitted olives, drained
4½ ounce jar white cocktail onions, drained
¾ cup olive oil
¼ cup salad oil
¼ cup **MINUTE MAID® 100% Pure Lemon Juice**
1¼ cups white wine vinegar
¼ cup sugar
2 teaspoons salt
¾ teaspoon ground pepper
1 clove garlic, minced

Mix vegetables together in a shallow dish. Bring remaining ingredients to a boil, cook five minutes and pour over vegetables. Cover and marinate for 24 hours in the refrigerator. Drain and serve with toothpicks.

Wheat Germ Zucchini Appetizers

3 cups thinly sliced zucchini
1 cup grated Parmesan cheese
¾ cup **KRETSCHMER Regular Wheat Germ**
4 eggs, slightly beaten
½ cup chopped onion
½ cup snipped parsley
¼ cup butter or margarine, melted
1 small clove garlic, minced
1 tsp. marjoram leaves, crushed
¼ tsp. salt
¼ tsp. pepper

Combine . . all ingredients, mixing well.
Spread . . . in greased 13x9x2-inch pan.
Bake . . . . . at 350° for 15-20 minutes until set.
Cool . . . . . about 5 minutes. Cut into small pieces. Serve warm.

Makes 4-5 dozen appetizers

Note: Appetizers may be reheated at 350° for 5-8 minutes or in the microwave about 1 minute.

Soups

Italian Stew

2 cups frozen **MU TOFU**, thawed and cubed
2 cups zucchini, cubed
1½ cups onions
2 cloves minced garlic
1 cup celery
1 28 oz. can tomatoes
⅓ cup soy sauce
2 bay leaves
1 Tbsp. basil
¼ tsp. rosemary
¼ tsp. savory
Dash pepper

Sauté onions, celery, and garlic in oil. Add tofu, zucchini, and tomatoes. Cook 4 minutes. Add spices, juice from tomatoes, and soy sauce. Simmer 1 hour.

Hamburger Helper®

Quick Italian Soup

1 pound ground beef
1 medium onion, chopped (about ½ cup)
1 package **BETTY CROCKER® HAMBURGER HELPER® Mix for Lasagne**
5 cups water
2 tablespoons grated Parmesan cheese
1 can (16 ounces) whole tomatoes, undrained
1 can (8¼ ounces) whole kernel corn, undrained
1 small zucchini, chopped (about 1 cup)

Cook and stir ground beef and onion in Dutch oven until beef is brown; drain. Stir in Sauce Mix, water, cheese, tomatoes and corn; break up tomatoes with fork. Heat to boiling, stirring constantly. Reduce heat; cover and simmer, stirring occasionally, 10 minutes. Stir in zucchini and Noodles; cover and cook 10 minutes longer. Sprinkle each serving with grated Parmesan cheese if desired.   *5 or 6 servings (about 9 cups soup)*

HIGH ALTITUDE DIRECTIONS (3500 to 6500 feet): Stir in Noodles and zucchini with the Sauce Mix. Continue as directed except—cover and simmer, stirring occasionally, 25 to 30 minutes.

Campbell's

Italiano Main Dish Soup

½ pound ground beef
½ cup chopped onion
1 medium clove garlic, minced
½ teaspoon oregano leaves, crushed
2 tablespoons shortening
2 cups coarsely chopped cabbage
1 can (11½ ounces) **CAMPBELL'S Condensed Bean with Bacon Soup**
1 soup can water
1 can (11½ ounces) **CAMPBELL'S Condensed Minestrone Soup**
1 can (about 8 ounces) kidney beans, drained
½ teaspoon salt
Generous dash pepper

Shape beef into 18 meatballs. In large saucepan, brown meatballs and cook onion with garlic and oregano in shortening until tender. Add cabbage; cook until just tender. Add bean with bacon soup; gradually stir in water. Add remaining ingredients. Heat; stir occasionally. Recipe may be doubled.   *Makes about 6 cups*

My Secret Minestrone Soup

1 medium onion, chopped
1 Tbsp. salad oil
1-16 oz. can whole tomatoes and juice, slightly chopped
1 small zucchini, sliced (optional)
½ tsp. chopped parsley
1 tsp. salt
½ cup elbow macaroni, cooked according to package
Grated Parmesan cheese, to pass (optional)
1 clove garlic minced
½ lb. left over cooked roast beef (chuck or any cut), cut into ½ inch cubes (lean pork roast may be substituted)
3 cups water
¼ tsp. ground marjoram
¼ tsp. black pepper
1-16 oz. can **VEG-ALL® Mixed Vegetables**, with liquid

In a large soup kettle, lightly sauté the onion and garlic in oil. Add the beef, tomatoes, zucchini, water and seasonings. Stir; bring to a boil; cover and reduce heat. Simmer for 15 minutes. Meanwhile cook the macaroni in another kettle. Drain. Add macaroni and **VEG-ALL®** to the soup kettle. Stir; heat through for 3 minutes.

Serve immediately in soup bowls. If desired, Parmesan cheese may be sprinkled on top.   *Serves 6*

Minestrone
(Italian Vegetable Soup)

1 cup dried beans
5 cups water
1 tablespoon minced onion
1 teaspoon parsley
½ cup chopped celery
½ clove garlic, minced
½ green pepper, diced
½ red pepper, diced
¼ cup olive oil
Thyme to taste
½ teaspoon salt
⅛ teaspoon pepper
1 cup diced cooked potatoes
1 cup chopped cabbage
½ cup cooked macaroni
1 cup **ENRICO'S Spaghetti Sauce**
Grated Parmesan cheese or any Italian style cheese

Soak beans overnight, drain. Add water, cover and simmer 2 or 3 hours or until tender. Add water as necessary. Sauté onion, parsley, celery, garlic, and peppers in oil. Add to beans with crushed thyme, salt, pepper, remaining vegetables and macaroni. Simmer 30 minutes more. Add **ENRICO'S Spaghetti Sauce** and simmer for 5 minutes more. Serve in soup bowls and sprinkle cheese over top. *Serves 6*

Easy Minestrone

In a large deep kettle cook and stir *2 pounds ground beef, crumbled,* until meat loses its pink color.

Add *2 onions, thinly sliced, 1 cup chopped celery* and *3 cloves garlic, crushed.* Cook, stirring occasionally, until onion is soft.

Add *2 cans pinto beans (15 oz. each) and their liquid, 1 large can (29 oz.) tomato puree, 2 teaspoons salt, 1½ teaspoons Italian herb seasoning* and *3 cups* **ALMADÉN Barbera**. Bring to boiling, cover, reduce heat and simmer for 45 minutes.

Stir in *2 packages (10 oz. each) frozen spinach, thawed and drained,* bring again to boiling and boil gently for 10 minutes longer.

Serve with additional **Barbera** to add to soup to taste and *grated Parmesan cheese* to sprinkle over.

Makes 6 to 8 servings

Italian Minestrone Soup

2½ lb. blade chuck roast or meaty soup bones
2½ qts. water
2 teaspoons salt
1 small onion, sliced
½ cup celery leaves
1 bay leaf

In a large pan, place all ingredients, cover and simmer about 2½ hours until meat is tender. Strain broth (should measure 2 quarts). Add ice cubes to harden the fat, and remove fat from broth. Finely dice meat, discarding fat and bones, to about 2 cups. In 5- or 6-qt. kettle, combine beef broth and meat. Place over low heat while preparing the following:

2 slices bacon, diced
1½ cups cooked or canned kidney beans
½ cup cut-up fresh green beans
½ cup diced celery
½ cup fresh or frozen green peas
½ cup thinly sliced zucchini
½ cup thinly sliced carrots
¼ cup diced onion
¼ cup cut-up parsley
1 clove garlic, minced
½ cup (2 oz.) elbow macaroni
1 can (6 oz.) tomato paste
1 cup **COCA-COLA®**
1 tablespoon olive oil
1 tablespoon Worcestershire sauce
1 teaspoon Italian seasoning
1 teaspoon salt
¼ teaspoon black pepper

Pan fry bacon until crisp. Add bacon with drippings and all the remaining ingredients to the broth. Cover and simmer about 30 minutes, until vegetables and macaroni are tender. Serve sprinkled with Parmesan cheese, if desired. *Makes about 3 quarts*

Tomato Zucchini Soup

2 cups unpeeled, diced zucchini
½ cup chopped onion
1 tablespoon olive oil
4 cups tomato juice
1 14½-ounce can chicken broth
3 tablespoons **HENRI'S TAS-TEE® Dressing**
2 tablespoons lime juice
1 teaspoon sugar
½ teaspoon salt
⅛ teaspoon hot pepper sauce
Parsley for garnish

1. In 2-quart saucepan, sauté zucchini and onion in olive oil.
2. Add tomato juice, chicken broth, **HENRI'S TAS-TEE® Dressing,** lime juice, sugar, salt, and hot pepper sauce.
3. Cover and simmer until vegetables are tender. Serve hot. Garnish with parsley. *Makes 6 ½-cup servings*

Ronzoni®

Stracciatella Soup

1 quart beef or chicken broth or bouillon
2 eggs
⅛ teaspoon salt
1½ tablespoons semolina
2 tablespoons **RONZONI® Grated Parmesan Cheese**

Combine eggs, salt, semolina, cheese and 3 tablespoons cool broth in mixing bowl and beat with fork 5 minutes. Bring rest of broth to boiling point and add egg mixture slowly, stirring constantly. Continue stirring while soup simmers 5 minutes.

Serves 4

Pasta in Broth with Vegetables

¼ cup chopped onions
5 tablespoons butter or margarine
2 tablespoons chopped parsley
1 can (15 oz.) CHEF BOY-AR-DEE® Cheese Ravioli in Sauce
1 cup water
1 packet G. WASHINGTON'S® Seasoning & Broth
1 cup chopped red pepper
1 package (10 oz.) frozen corn, cooked and drained
1 cup sliced mushrooms
½ package (10 oz.) chopped broccoli, cooked and drained

Sauté chopped onions in 1 tablespoon butter. Combine onions, parsley, Cheese Ravioli in Sauce, water and G. WASHINGTON'S® Seasoning and Broth in a 2-quart saucepan. Cover; simmer for 10 minutes. Meantime, sauté each vegetable separately adding more butter as needed; remove each to small individual bowls or dishes. Garnish with broccoli or serve it as other vegetables.

Serve soup with these or other favored vegetables on the side as garnishes. Diners may choose which vegetables they prefer for adding to soup.

Serves 4

Neapolitan Bean Stew

(Pasta Fagioli Alla Napoli)

8 oz. dried white beans
3 Tablespoons olive oil
1 cup chopped onions
3 oz. prosciutto ham, finely diced
1 cup chopped celery
2 teaspoons salt
½ teaspoon oregano
⅛ teaspoon black pepper
1 10¼ oz. can BUITONI® Marinara Sauce
1 package BUITONI® Ditali No. 35
BUITONI® Grated Parmesan Cheese

Wash beans and soak overnight in generous amount of water. Brown onions in olive oil, then add prosciutto and simmer gently one minute. In a large pot combine drained beans, celery, seasonings, onions and prosciutto with 2½ qts. cold water. Cover and simmer gently for about one hour, until beans are tender. Add Sauce and Ditali and boil 6 minutes longer. Serve in soup bowls and sprinkle with grated Parmesan cheese.

3-4 one cup servings

Salads

Luncheon Salad

(Low Calorie)

1 (7 ounce) package or 2 cups uncooked CREAMETTES® Elbow Macaroni, cooked as package directs, rinsed and drained
1 (7 ounce) can tuna packed in water, drained and flaked
4 slices low calorie cheese, cut into small pieces
½ cup chopped green pepper
2 tablespoons chopped pimiento
6 tablespoons bottled low calorie Italian dressing
2 tablespoons lemon juice
1 to 2 tablespoons prepared horseradish
½ teaspoon garlic salt
2 tablespoons chopped parsley
8 medium tomatoes (cut into wedges, cutting to, but not through, bases)

In large bowl, combine all ingredients except tomatoes; mix well. Chill thoroughly. Serve in tomatoes. Refrigerate leftovers.

Makes 8 servings

Calories: Prepared as directed, provides approximately 180 calories per serving.

VARIATION:

Add 2 cups chopped fresh tomatoes to salad mixture, serve on lettuce instead of in tomatoes.

Fisherman's Favorite Cioppino Salad

1 cup WISH-BONE® Italian Dressing
¼ cup dry white wine
¼ teaspoon dry basil or ¾ teaspoon chopped fresh basil
2 cups cooked Dungeness crabmeat (about ¾ lb.)
¾ pound large shrimp, cleaned and cooked
2 quarts mixed salad greens
3 cups coarsely chopped tomatoes
10 artichoke hearts, halved*
1 medium red onion, cut into rings

In large shallow baking dish, blend WISH-BONE® Italian Dressing, wine and basil; add crabmeat and shrimp. Cover and marinate in refrigerator, turning occasionally, at least 2 hours.

Meanwhile, in salad bowl, arrange salad greens, tomatoes, artichoke hearts and onion; chill. Just before serving, add seafood with marinade and toss. Garnish, if desired, with chopped parsley.

Makes 6 to 8 servings

*Substitution: Use 1 can (15 oz.) artichoke hearts, drained and halved.

Best Foods®/HELLMANN'S®

Pasta-Tuna Salad

1 cup **BEST FOODS®/HELLMANN'S® Real Mayonnaise**
2 tablespoons red wine vinegar
Dash pepper
4 ounces twist macaroni (1 cup), cooked, drained
1 can (7-oz.) tuna, drained, flaked
1 cup cooked peas
1 cup sliced celery
½ cup chopped red onion
¼ cup snipped dill or 1 tablespoon dried dill weed

In large bowl stir together Real Mayonnaise, vinegar and pepper until smooth. Add macaroni, tuna, peas, celery, onion and dill. Toss to coat well. Cover; refrigerate at least 2 hours to blend flavors. *Makes 4 servings*

VARIATION:

Pasta-Ham Salad

Follow recipe for Pasta-Tuna Salad. Substitute 1¼ cups diced cooked ham for tuna.

Italian Scallop Salad

¾ pound cooked scallops, fresh or frozen
1 can (16 ounces) cut green beans, drained
2 hard-cooked eggs, chopped
⅔ cup sliced celery
⅓ cup raw cauliflower "Flowerettes"
⅓ cup thinly sliced unpeeled cucumber
¼ cup sliced green pepper
1 teaspoon salt
½ teaspoon pepper
½ cup Italian salad dressing
¼ cup chopped pimiento (Optional)
Radish roses
Salad greens

Remove any remaining shell from cooked scallops. Cut large scallops in half. Combine all ingredients except radish roses and salad greens; toss lightly. Place about one cup salad on each salad plate which has been lined with salad greens. Garnish with radish roses. *Serves 6*

Favorite recipe from **National Marine Fisheries Service**

KNOX®

A Little Bit of Italy

4 envelopes **KNOX® Unflavored Gelatine**
5½ cups cold water
1½ cups **WISH-BONE® Italian Dressing**
1 can (7 oz.) tuna, drained and flaked
1 can (4 oz.) sliced mushrooms, drained
1½ cups chopped green pepper
½ cup sliced pitted ripe olives
⅓ cup diced pimiento

In large saucepan, sprinkle unflavored gelatine over 2 cups water; let stand 1 minute. Stir over low heat until gelatine is completely dissolved, about 5 minutes. Add remaining water and real Italian dressing. Pour into large bowl and chill, stirring occasionally, until mixture is consistency of unbeaten egg whites. Fold in remaining ingredients. Turn into 13 x 9 pan or individual molds; chill until firm. To serve, cut into squares or unmold and serve on lettuce-lined plates. Garnish, if desired, with salami and provolone cheese. *Makes about 20 servings*

Insalata con Tonno

3 tablespoons olive oil
2 tablespoons white wine vinegar
1 clove garlic, minced
½ teaspoon basil leaves, crushed
⅛ teaspoon dry mustard
Dash ground black pepper
1 can (6½ oz.) **CHICKEN OF THE SEA® Chunk Light Tuna,** drained and flaked*
2 cups torn salad greens
1 large firm ripe tomato, coarsely chopped
¼ cup sliced pitted ripe olives
¼ cup thinly sliced celery
¼ cup (1 oz.) diced mozzarella cheese

In small bowl combine olive oil, wine vinegar, garlic, basil, dry mustard and pepper. Mix well. Add tuna. Toss to coat. Cover. Refrigerate 2 to 3 hours. In large bowl combine salad greens, tomato, olives, celery and cheese. Stir tuna mixture; pour over greens. Toss to coat. *Makes 4 cups*

*Tuna packed in oil or water may be used, based on personal preference.

Linguine Tuna Salad

½ (1-pound) package **CREAMETTE® Linguine,** broken in half
¼ cup **REALEMON® Lemon Juice from Concentrate**
¼ cup vegetable oil
¼ cup chopped green onions
2 teaspoons sugar
1 teaspoon Italian seasoning
1 teaspoon seasoned salt
1 (12½-ounce) can tuna, drained
1 (10-ounce) package frozen green peas, thawed
2 cups chopped fresh tomatoes
Lettuce

Cook linguine according to package directions; drain. Meanwhile, in large bowl, combine remaining ingredients except tuna, peas and tomatoes; mix well. Add *hot* linguine; toss. Add remaining ingredients; mix well. Chill thoroughly. Serve on lettuce garnished as desired. Refrigerate leftovers. *Makes 6 servings*

Mazola.

Mediterranean Meatball Salad

¼ cup **MAZOLA® Corn Oil,** divided
2 tablespoons water
1 tablespoon lemon juice
1 teaspoon dried mint leaves
1 pound lean ground beef round
½ cup finely grated onion
½ cup soft whole wheat bread crumbs
3 tablespoons chopped parsley
½ teaspoon salt
¼ teaspoon pepper
1½ cups diagonally sliced carrots, cooked, drained
1 cup cubed green pepper
3 cups lightly packed torn salad greens
1 large tomato, cut in wedges

In small jar with tight fitting lid place 2 tablespoons of the corn oil, water, lemon juice and mint. Cover; shake well. Refrigerate at least 1 hour. In large bowl mix beef, onion, bread crumbs, parsley, salt and pepper until well blended. Shape into 1-inch meatballs. In large skillet heat remaining 2 tablespoons of the corn oil over medium heat. Add ½ of the meatballs; cook shaking pan often 10 minutes or until brown on all sides and cooked. Remove; drain well on paper towels. Brown remaining meatballs. In large bowl toss together meatballs, carrots and green pepper. Cover; refrigerate 1 hour. To serve, toss meatball mixture with dressing. Arrange on platter with salad greens and tomato.

Makes 6 servings

Low-Calorie Version: Follow recipe for Mediterranean Meatball Salad. Omit bread crumbs and remaining 2 tablespoons corn oil for browning meatballs. In large bowl mix beef, onion, parsley, 1 tablespoon prepared mustard, salt and pepper. Shape into 1-inch meatballs. Place on 15½ x 10½ x 1-inch jelly roll pan. Bake in 450°F oven 8 to 10 minutes, turning once, or until cooked and browned on all sides. Continue as in basic recipe.

Lima Garlic Salad

1 package (10 ounces) frozen lima beans, cooked and drained
1½ cups cherry tomatoes, cut in half
1 medium purple onion, sliced and separated into rings
1 medium green pepper, cored, seeded and cut into strips
½ cup sliced black olives
½ cup olive oil
2 tablespoons lemon juice
1 large clove garlic, minced
½ teaspoon salt
¼ teaspoon basil, crushed
1 cup **PEPPERIDGE FARM® Cheddar and Romano Croutons**
Lettuce leaves
Chopped parsley

In a large bowl, combine vegetables. Blend oil, lemon juice, garlic, salt and basil. Pour over vegetables; toss to blend. Cover and refrigerate at least 2 hours. To serve, spoon over lettuce leaves and sprinkle with croutons. Garnish with parsley.

Makes 4 to 6 servings

Italian Salad

1 medium can tiny whole green beans or French-cut cooked fresh beans
8-10 cherry tomatoes, halved
4 fresh green onions, sliced
½ cup French Dressing II*
BROWNBERRY® Seasoned Croutons

Drain the chilled green beans and gently mix together all ingredients except croutons. Chill at least one hour, or longer if more convenient. Toss in the croutons at serving time, and serve in an ice-cold lettuce lined bowl.

*French Dressing II

¼ cup olive oil
¼ cup peanut oil
¼ cup wine vinegar
1 tsp. paprika
1 tsp. salt
Garlic clove

Combine ingredients in glass jar and shake well. This is enough for a large tossed salad, but any remaining may be stored in refrigerator.

Artichoke Surprise Salad

7-oz. package **CREAMETTES® Macaroni,** (2 cups uncooked)
1 package (9 oz.) frozen artichoke hearts
1 can (5½-oz.) lobster, shrimp or crabmeat, drained and flaked
½ cup French dressing
½ cup mayonnaise
1 teaspoon salt
½ teaspoon basil
¼ teaspoon pepper
Lettuce
½ cup sliced radishes

Prepare **CREAMETTES®** according to package directions for salad use. Drain. Prepare artichoke hearts according to package directions. Drain. Combine all ingredients except lettuce and radishes. Chill. Serve in lettuce lined bowl. Garnish with radishes.

6 servings

Calories: 177 per serving

VARIATION:

One 7-oz. can tuna may be added. Water-packed tuna will increase calories to 219 per serving. Oil-packed tuna will increase calories to 242 per serving. Shrimp, crabmeat, ham or chicken may be added. Adjust the calories for the addition.

Antipasto in a Bowl

1 can **GOYA® Chick Peas,** drained and rinsed
½ cup salami, diced
½ cup celery, chopped
½ cup black olives, chopped
½ cup green pepper, strips
2 pimientos, chopped
½ tsp. salt
½ tsp. black pepper
¼ tsp. chili powder
2 Tbsp. salad oil
1 Tbsp. red wine vinegar

Combine all ingredients in large bowl. Toss well, cover and chill before serving.

Campbell's

Antipasto Salad

Marinade:
1 can (10¾ ounces) **CAMPBELL'S Condensed Tomato Soup**
½ cup salad oil
½ cup wine vinegar
1 package (0.6 ounces) mild Italian salad dressing mix

Vegetables:
2 cups diagonally sliced carrots
2 cups small cauliflowerets
2 cups cubed zucchini squash
1 cup small fresh mushroom caps
½ cup pimiento-stuffed olives
½ cup sliced pepperoni
1 medium green pepper, cut in strips

In saucepan, combine marinade ingredients; bring to boil. Reduce heat; simmer 5 minutes. Stir occasionally. In 3-quart shallow baking dish (13x9x2-inch), arrange vegetables. Pour marinade over vegetables. Chill 6 hours or more; stir occasionally. Serve with slotted spoon.   *Makes about 8 cups, 10 servings*

Cool and Green Rice Salad

1 bag **SUCCESS® Rice**
2 small or 1 large zucchini
1 or 2 green onions, sliced
3 tablespoons bottled creamy Italian dressing
¼ teaspoon black pepper
1 avocado
1 tablespoon lemon juice

Cook bag of rice according to cooking directions; but cook 20 minutes. During last five minutes, gently place the zucchini on top

of the bag and let steam. With tongs, remove zucchini to cutting board. Cut off ends and slice zucchini into ¼-inch pieces. Drain bag and empty rice into mixing bowl. Add the zucchini, green onion, dressing, and black pepper. Chill. Just before serving, peel the avocado, slice and dip in the lemon juice. Arrange around the salad or gently toss with it.

Makes 6 servings (about ½ cup each)

Calories: 174 calories per serving

claussen

Marinated Fresh Vegetables

Heat juice from 1 jar **CLAUSSEN Kosher Pickles** (about 2 cups). Arrange fresh vegetables—cherry tomatoes, celery, carrots, cauliflower and broccoli in empty pickle jar. Pour heated juice over vegetables and replace lid. Refrigerate vegetables 24 hours before serving.

Mediterranean Spring Salad

½ pound new potatoes or other fresh potatoes
½ cup olive oil
2 tablespoons fresh lemon juice
1 clove garlic, crushed
2 teaspoons oregano
¼ teaspoon salt
6 cups coarsely cut, mixed salad greens (lettuce, romaine, chickory or escarole)
1 large fresh tomato, cut in wedges
1 medium green pepper, seeded and thinly sliced
1 small red onion, thinly sliced
1 small cucumber, thinly sliced
½ cup feta cheese, cubed
1 can (2 ounces) flat fillets of anchovies

Cook potatoes, covered, in boiling, salted water to cover, until tender, about 25 minutes. Drain; pare and slice. In small bowl or jar, combine olive oil, lemon juice, garlic, oregano and salt; mix well; pour over potatoes; allow to marinate 1 hour. Place salad greens in salad bowl. Drain potatoes; reserve dressing. Arrange potatoes, tomato, green pepper, red onion, cucumber, feta cheese and anchovies over greens. Serve with reserved dressing.

Makes: 6 servings

Favorite recipe from **United Fresh Fruit & Vegetable Association**

Salad Italiano

1 jar (6 ounces) marinated artichoke hearts, undrained
¼ cup sliced green onions
Juice of 1 fresh **SUNKIST® Lemon**
1 small head romaine lettuce, torn in bite-size pieces
1 small head Bibb or Boston lettuce, torn in bite-size pieces
2 tomatoes, cut in wedges
1 small zucchini, thinly sliced

To make dressing, combine undrained artichoke hearts, green onions and lemon juice; chill. In large salad bowl, combine remaining ingredients; chill. To serve, pour dressing over salad mixture; toss well. *Makes 6 servings*

VARIATION:
Combine undrained artichoke hearts, green onions and lemon juice. Serve on crisp salad greens. *Makes about 1 cup*

Zucchini Toss

1 medium head iceberg lettuce, torn into bite-size
  pieces
1 small bunch romaine, torn into bite-size pieces
2 medium zucchini, thinly sliced
3 green onions (with tops), sliced
1 cup sliced radishes
½ cup **BAC*OS®** Imitation Bacon
3 tablespoons crumbled blue cheese, if desired
½ cup bottled Italian dressing

Toss all ingredients except dressing. Pour dressing over salad; toss. Sprinkle with 1 to 2 tablespoons imitation bacon if desired.
6 to 8 servings

Vegetable Pepperoni Salad

1 package (16 ounces) **Frozen STOKELY'S®**
  Vegetables Milano®
1 medium-size head lettuce, torn
2 tomatoes, cut in wedges (optional)
4 ounces mozzarella cheese, cubed
2 hard-cooked eggs, diced
½ cup thinly sliced pepperoni
¼ cup sliced scallion (green onion)
2 Tablespoons sliced black olives
½ cup Italian dressing
Salt and pepper to taste
1 jar (4 ounces) **STOKELY'S FINEST®** Sliced
  Pimientos, drained

Cook frozen vegetables according to package directions, drain, and cool. In a large salad bowl, combine all ingredients except dressing, salt, pepper, and pimientos. Toss mixture lightly with dressing, season to taste, and garnish with pimientos. *8 servings*

Heinz

Chilled Vegetable Medley

½ cup **HEINZ Wine Vinegar**
¼ cup salad oil
¾ teaspoon salt
½ teaspoon oregano leaves
⅛ teaspoon pepper
2 tomatoes, cut into chunks
1 cucumber, sliced
1 cup sliced celery
1 medium onion, sliced
¼ cup sliced pitted ripe olives
¼ cup broken walnuts

Combine first 5 ingredients in jar; shake vigorously. Pour marinade over tomatoes and remaining ingredients. Cover; chill several hours, tossing occasionally. Salad may be served on a bed of shredded lettuce, if desired. *Makes 6 servings (5 cups)*

Insalada Pepperidge

3 cups new potatoes, unpeeled, cooked and sliced
2 small zucchini, sliced (about 1½ cups)
1 cup sliced celery
2 medium tomatoes, cut in wedges
½ cup sliced stuffed olives
½ cup olive oil
3 tablespoons wine vinegar
¼ cup chopped parsley
½ teaspoon salt
¼ teaspoon oregano, crushed
⅛ teaspoon pepper
1 cup **PEPPERIDGE FARM®** Onion and Garlic
  Croutons
3 tablespoons grated Parmesan cheese
Lettuce leaves

In a bowl, combine vegetables. Combine oil, vinegar, parsley and seasonings and mix well. Pour over vegetables; toss to blend. Cover and refrigerate at least 2 hours. To serve, spoon over lettuce leaves and sprinkle with onion and garlic croutons. Sprinkle with grated Parmesan cheese. *Makes 6 to 8 servings*

Creamy Italian Dressing

1 cup **BEST FOODS®/HELLMANN'S®** Real
  Mayonnaise
½ small onion
2 tablespoons red wine vinegar
1 tablespoon sugar
¾ teaspoon Italian seasoning
¼ teaspoon salt
¼ teaspoon garlic salt or powder
⅛ teaspoon pepper

Place all ingredients in blender container; cover. Blend until smooth. Cover; chill. *Makes 1¼ cups*

Caesar Salad

2 medium heads romaine lettuce
3 to 4 anchovy fillets
6 tablespoons salad oil
1 egg
1 tablespoon Worcestershire sauce
¼ teaspoon salt
Dash freshly ground pepper
¼ cup grated Parmesan cheese
Juice from 2 lemons (4 tablespoons)
2 cups garlic croutons

Tear romaine into medium-sized pieces and put into large salad bowl. Mash anchovies in small bowl. Pour in 3 tablespoons of the salad oil; add egg, Worcestershire sauce, salt and pepper. Whip together with fork. Toss greens with remaining 3 tablespoons salad oil and Parmesan cheese. Add egg-anchovy mixture and lightly toss again. Sprinkle with lemon juice, toss lightly. Add croutons; toss lightly. Serve salad immediately while croutons are still crisp.

Favorite recipe from **Leafy Greens Council**

Morton Caesar Salad

12 cups torn romaine lettuce leaves (about 1½ pounds)
¼ cup olive oil
2 tablespoons lemon juice (about 1 medium lemon)
1 medium garlic clove
½ teaspoon **MORTON Table Salt**
¼ teaspoon dry mustard
⅛ teaspoon coarse black pepper
1 cup unseasoned croutons
¼ cup grated Parmesan cheese
1 egg, beaten
1 can (2 ounces) anchovy fillets, rolled

Early in Day: Place lettuce in large salad bowl; cover with wet paper towels and refrigerate. Combine oil, lemon juice, garlic, table salt, mustard, and pepper. Cover and let stand until serving time.

Just Before Serving: Remove garlic clove. Stir dressing well. Add dressing to salad; toss lightly. Add croutons and cheese; toss. Add egg; toss well. Garnish with rolled anchovy fillets. Serve immediately. *Makes 8 servings*

Cheez-It® Caesar Salad

⅓ cup salad oil
3 tablespoons lemon juice
½ teaspoon salt
⅛ teaspoon pepper
1 small head chicory
1 small head romaine lettuce
1 small head escarole
16 **CHEEZ-IT® Crackers**
1 small garlic bud, halved
1 raw egg

Combine salad oil, lemon juice, salt and pepper in small bowl. Wash chicory, romaine and escarole, and remove any limp outer leaves. Break or cut greens into 2 inch pieces, discarding tough spines. Rub **CHEEZ-IT® Crackers** with surface of garlic. Also rub inside of a large wooden salad bowl with garlic. Arrange greens in garlic-rubbed bowl. Break the raw egg over the salad and add crackers, broken in half. Stir oil-lemon juice dressing to blend well; pour over salad and toss with salad fork and spoon until greens are well coated with egg and dressing.
Yield: 6 to 8 generous servings

Pasta

Armanino Farms of *California*

Pasta al Pesto

For a delicious Pasta al Pesto simply use **ARMANINO FARMS** Ready to use **Frozen Pesto** from the 4-ounce package or make

Pesto from the **Freeze-dried** packet according to package directions and blend either into a 12-ounce package of cooked and drained flat noodles. Top with grated Parmesan or Romano cheese and serve as a dinner accompaniment or main dish.

VARIATIONS:

1. Add cooked small bay shrimp or shredded crab or lobster meat for a satisfying entree.
2. Instead of flat noodles try Pesto on any cooked spaghetti, macaroni shape or rice.

Ham and Noodles Tonnarelli

Dice:
    ½ lb. cooked ham

Drain, reserving liquid for other recipes:
    1 can (16 oz.) **DEL MONTE Sweet Peas**
    1 can (4 oz.) sliced mushrooms

Cook as package directs:
    2 cups egg noodles

Drain.

Using same saucepan, melt:
    ¼ cup butter or margarine

Add ham and mushrooms; heat. Add noodles and peas; heat.

Toss lightly with:
    ¾ cup Parmesan cheese

Serve in warm serving dish, garnished with sprigs of fresh parsley.

Noodles Primavera

½ (12-oz.) pkg. **AMERICAN BEAUTY® Wide Egg Noodles**
¼ cup butter or margarine
1 clove garlic, minced
1 cup chopped onions
1 cup thinly sliced carrots
1 cup frozen peas
1 small bunch fresh broccoli, cut into 1-inch pieces, or 10-oz. pkg. frozen chopped broccoli, thawed and drained
4½-oz. or 2 (2½-oz.) jars **GREEN GIANT® Whole Mushrooms**, drained
½ teaspoon basil leaves
¼ teaspoon seasoned salt
1 medium zucchini, cut into 1½-inch lengths and quartered
Grated Parmesan cheese

Cook noodles to desired doneness as directed on package. In large skillet, melt butter over low heat. Stir in garlic and onions; sauté for 2 minutes. Add remaining ingredients except zucchini and Parmesan cheese; sauté until tender-crisp, about 5 minutes, stirring occasionally. Add zucchini; sauté an additional 5 minutes. Combine cooked noodles and vegetables; toss lightly. If desired, sprinkle with Parmesan cheese. *8 (1-cup) servings*

HIGH ALTITUDE—Above 3500 feet: Cooking time may need to be increased slightly for noodles.

Tuna Casserole

1 box **GOODMAN Broad Egg Noodles**
1 bunch scallions
1 13 oz. can of tuna fish
Parmesan cheese (grated)
2 sliced mushrooms
2 cups cream

Cook egg noodles 6 to 8 minutes. Set aside. Sauté scallions in 4 oz. of butter, until translucent. Place in bowl. Add tuna fish, 3 Tbsp. Parmesan cheese, sliced mushrooms and cream. Season with salt and pepper. Layer in baking dish between noodles and top with 3 Tbsp. Parmesan cheese. Bake at 350° for 25-30 minutes. Let rest 5 minutes before serving.

R·F® Mostaccioli with Beefy Tomato Sauce

2 Tbsp. olive oil
1 sliced onion
1 clove garlic, minced
¼ cup celery, diced
1 pound ground beef
1 can plum tomatoes (1 pound-12 ounce size)
1 can tomato sauce (8 ounces)
½ tsp. salt
¼ tsp. each basil, oregano, thyme
¼ cup dry red wine
8 ounces **R·F® Mostaccioli**
Grated Parmesan cheese

In a large skillet, sauté the onion, garlic and celery in the olive oil until onion is transparent. Push vegetables to one side and brown the ground beef. Add the tomatoes (breaking into smaller pieces with edge of spoon), tomato sauce, wine and seasonings. Simmer for 20 minutes.

Meanwhile, cook the Mostaccioli in boiling, salted water as directed on package. Drain. Mix the sauce with the Mostaccioli. Serve with plenty of grated Parmesan cheese.   *Serves 4*

Lipton.

Souper Skillet Ziti

1 pound ground beef
1 envelope **LIPTON® Beef Flavor Mushroom** or **Onion-Mushroom Soup Mix**
2 cans (16 oz. ea.) whole tomatoes, undrained
2 cups water
1½ teaspoons oregano
3 cups uncooked ziti macaroni (about 8 oz.)
⅓ cup grated Parmesan cheese
Mozzarella cheese

In large skillet, brown ground beef; drain. Add beef flavor mushroom soup mix and tomatoes blended with water and oregano. Bring to a boil, then stir in uncooked macaroni; simmer covered, stirring occasionally, 20 minutes or until macaroni is tender. Stir in Parmesan cheese and top with mozzarella cheese.

Makes about 6 servings

Top Ramen.

Roman Ramen

Before opening break-up noodles in 2 pkg. **Onion Flavor TOP RAMEN.** Add noodles to 2 cups boiling water. Cook uncovered, stir occasionally for 3 minutes. Cook 8 oz. Italian sausage with seasonings from both flavor packets until crumbly. Stir in 16 oz. stewed tomatoes, 4 oz. jar drained sliced mushrooms, and ½ tsp. Italian seasonings. Simmer 2 minutes. Serve over hot noodles. Garnish with grated Parmesan cheese and parsley.   *Serves 4*

Sealtest®

Noodles Romanoff

4 chicken or beef bouillon cubes
4 cups boiling water
8 ounces fine noodles
1½ cups **SEALTEST® Cottage Cheese**
1 cup **SEALTEST® Sour Cream**
1 small onion, minced
½ teaspoon salt
¼ teaspoon thyme
¼ teaspoon garlic salt
½ cup bread crumbs

Dissolve chicken or beef bouillon cubes in boiling water. Cook noodles in broth until tender. Do not drain. Stir cottage cheese, sour cream, onion and seasonings into hot cooked undrained noodles. Mix until blended. Turn into a shallow 10-cup baking dish. Top with crumbs. Bake, uncovered, in a preheated 350° oven for 25 minutes. Serve hot.   *6 servings*

Tagliarini with Gallo® Salame Sauce

½ cup **GALLO® Italian Dry Salame** strips (cut julienne style)
1 medium-sized onion, chopped
¼ cup butter
2 ounces cooked ham, cut julienne style
1 package (10 oz.) tagliarini noodles or other fresh egg noodles
2 egg yolks, lightly beaten
⅓ cup chopped parsley
1 green onion, chopped
¾ cup diced Gruyère or Monterey Jack cheese
1 cup freshly grated Parmesan cheese
Freshly ground pepper, to taste

Sauté onion in 1 tablespoon of butter until glazed. Add **GALLO® Salame** and ham and heat through. Melt remaining butter. Cook pasta as directed in boiling salted water 2 min. until tender. Drain, place in a bowl. Pour over melted butter, egg yolks, **GALLO® Salame** mixture, parsley, green onion, diced cheese and half the Parmesan. Mix until noodles are coated. Grind pepper over. Pass remaining Parmesan at table.   *Serves 4*

Pasta Verdura

2 tablespoons olive oil
1 medium onion, thinly sliced
1 package (1½ oz.) LAWRY'S® Spaghetti Sauce Mix
    with Imported Mushrooms
1 can (8 oz.) tomato sauce
1½ cups water
½ cup olive oil
4 zucchini, cut into ½-inch slices
1 small eggplant, peeled, thinly sliced and each slice
    quartered
1 medium green bell pepper, cut into 1-inch squares
3 medium tomatoes, cut into wedges
1½ tablespoons LAWRY'S® Seasoned Salt
½ pound noodles or spaghetti, cooked according to
    package instructions, drained and buttered to
    taste
¼ pound Mozzarella cheese, grated

In medium skillet, heat 2 tablespoons oil and sauté onion. Add **Spaghetti Sauce Mix with Imported Mushrooms**, tomato sauce and water. Bring to boil, reduce heat and simmer for 5 minutes; set aside. In large skillet, heat ½ cup oil and sauté zucchini, eggplant, green pepper and tomatoes. Add hot spaghetti sauce and Seasoned Salt to vegetables. Mix carefully and continue to cook over low heat for 20 minutes. To serve, top noodles with hot vegetables and sauce; sprinkle with grated cheese.

Makes 6 servings

Aunt Nellie's®

Beef and Cheese Stuffed Pasta

20 large pasta shells
1 pound ground beef
¼ cup chopped onion
1 clove garlic, crushed
½ teaspoon salt
¼ teaspoon pepper
2 cups (8 ounces) shredded low moisture part-skim
    mozzarella cheese
1 can (15½ ounces) AUNT NELLIE'S® Sloppy Joe
    Sandwich Sauce
¾ cup beef bouillon
Grated Parmesan cheese

Cook pasta according to package directions. Meanwhile, brown beef with onion and garlic. Remove from heat; drain. Season with salt and pepper. Add mozzarella cheese to slightly cooled meat; mix well. Combine sandwich sauce and bouillon; pour ¾ cup into 12 x 7½ x 2-inch baking dish. Fill shells with beef and cheese mixture; arrange in dish. Pour remaining sauce mixture over shells. Cover tightly. Bake at 350° for 35 to 40 minutes or until bubbly. Sprinkle with Parmesan cheese before serving.

4 to 5 servings

Wyler's®
Italian Stuffed Shells

24 CREAMETTE® Jumbo Macaroni Shells, cooked
    and drained
1 tablespoon WYLER'S® Beef-Flavor Instant
    Bouillon OR 3 Beef-Flavor Bouillon Cubes
2 cups boiling water
1 pound lean ground beef
⅔ cup chopped onion
1 clove garlic, chopped
2 (6-ounce) cans tomato paste
1½ teaspoons oregano leaves
1 (15-ounce) container ricotta cheese
2 cups (8 ounces) shredded mozzarella cheese
½ cup grated Parmesan cheese
1 egg

Dissolve bouillon in water; set aside. In large skillet, brown beef, onion and garlic. Stir in tomato paste, oregano and bouillon liquid; simmer 30 minutes. In medium bowl, combine ricotta, 1 cup mozzarella, grated cheese and egg; mix well. Stuff shells with cheese mixture; arrange in individual ramekins or 13x9-inch baking dish. Pour sauce over shells; cover. Bake in preheated 350° oven 30 minutes. Uncover; sprinkle with remaining mozzarella. Bake 3 minutes longer. Refrigerate leftovers.

Makes 6 to 8 servings

Buitoni® Shrimp Marinara

2 tablespoons olive oil
2 cloves garlic, minced
1 lb. uncooked shrimp, peeled and deveined
1 10¼ oz. can BUITONI® Marinara Sauce
1 Tablespoon chopped parsley
1 pinch oregano
¼ teaspoon salt
1 pkg. BUITONI® Shells
BUITONI® Grated Parmesan Cheese

In a large skillet, brown garlic lightly in olive oil. Add shrimp, cover, and cook gently 5 minutes. Add Sauce, parsley and seasonings and mix well. Simmer covered 5 minutes more.

Cook Shells according to package directions. Drain and place on warmed serving dish. Top with hot Shrimp Sauce and sprinkle with Parmesan Cheese. *3-4 One Cup Servings*

Manicotti Shrimp Marinara

¾ pound peeled, deveined shrimp, fresh or frozen
1 package (10 ounces) frozen, chopped spinach
⅓ cup margarine or butter, melted
1½ teaspoons Worcestershire sauce
½ teaspoon celery salt
½ teaspoon salt
¼ teaspoon liquid hot pepper sauce
1½ cups chopped lettuce
½ cup chopped green onion and tops
½ cup chopped parsley
2 cloves garlic, minced
½ cup dry curd cottage cheese
1 egg, beaten
8 (4 ounces) manicotti
1 jar (32 ounces) thick spaghetti sauce
2 tablespoons Parmesan cheese

Thaw shrimp if frozen. Thaw spinach and drain. Blend seasonings into margarine. Add vegetables and simmer for 10 minutes or until tender. Add cottage cheese and egg to vegetable mixture. Prepare manicotti according to package directions. Fill manicotti shells with equal amounts of vegetable stuffing. Spread 1 cup of spaghetti sauce over bottom of shallow 1½ quart casserole. Arrange stuffed manicotti on sauce in casserole. Spoon an additional 1 cup of spaghetti sauce over stuffed manicotti. Combine remaining spaghetti sauce and shrimp. Cover dish with aluminum foil, crimping it to edges of dish. Bake in moderate oven, 350°F, for 30 minutes. Uncover and spread shrimp mixture over stuffed shells. Bake 15 to 20 minutes longer or until shrimp are opaque in the center when cut with a knife. Sprinkle Parmesan cheese over top when removed from oven. *Makes 8 servings*

Favorite recipe from **Florida Department of Natural Resources**

Manicotti with Four Cheeses

½ cup butter or margarine
1 large onion, minced
1 lb. mushrooms, sliced
½ cup flour
4 cups milk
1 cup **SARGENTO Grated Parmesan and Romano Blend Cheese**
Salt and pepper
12 manicotti shells
15 oz. **SARGENTO Ricotta Cheese**
1 cup (4 oz.) **SARGENTO Shredded Cheese for Pizza (Mozzarella)**
1 cup **SARGENTO Grated Parmesan and Romano Blend Cheese**
½ cup finely chopped walnuts
¼ cup chopped parsley
3 eggs
Dash nutmeg

In a saucepan melt butter and sauté onion and mushrooms for 5 minutes. Stir in flour. Gradually stir in milk. Stir over low heat until sauce bubbles and thickens. Stir in Parmesan/Romano cheese, salt, and pepper to taste. Set aside. Cook manicotti shells according to package directions. Drain and cover with cold water. In a bowl, mix ricotta, mozzarella, grated cheese, walnuts, parsley, and eggs. Season to taste with salt, pepper and a dash of nutmeg. Drain manicotti noodles and stuff with cheese mixture. Place shells side by side in a greased shallow baking dish. Spoon sauce over. Bake in a preheated hot oven (400°F) for 20 to 25 minutes or until bubbly and lightly brown. Makes 12 manicotti.

Serves 6

Low-Calorie Manicotti

12 manicotti shells
1 container (8 ounces) dry-curd cottage cheese
1 container (8 ounces) part-skim ricotta cheese
1 cup (about 4 ounces) grated mozzarella cheese
2 eggs
½ cup low-fat milk
2 packets **BUTTER BUDS**®
¼ cup chopped fresh parsley
1 teaspoon oregano
½ teaspoon garlic powder
¼ teaspoon white pepper
Tomato Sauce*

Preheat oven to 350°F. Prepare manicotti shells according to package directions. Drain. Cool quickly in cool water. In large bowl, combine cheeses, eggs, and milk and mix well. Blend in **BUTTER BUDS**®, parsley, oregano, garlic powder, and pepper. Stuff shells with cheese mixture. Coat bottom of baking dish with Tomato Sauce. Place filled manicotti shells on top of sauce. Cover shells with remaining sauce. Bake, covered, 40 to 45 minutes.

6 servings

PER SERVING (2 shells): Calories: 275 Protein: 17gm
Carbohydrate: 37gm   Fat: 5gm   Sodium: 660mg

Note: By using **BUTTER BUDS**® instead of butter in this recipe, you have saved 250 calories and 93 mg cholesterol per serving.

*Tomato Sauce

1 tablespoon vegetable oil
½ cup chopped green pepper
½ cup (1 medium-size) chopped onion
2 medium-size garlic cloves, minced
1 can (1 pound 12 ounces) peeled tomatoes, chopped
½ cup water
1 can (6 ounces) tomato paste
¼ cup chopped fresh parsley
1 packet **BUTTER BUDS**®, made into liquid
1 teaspoon basil
1 teaspoon thyme
¼ teaspoon freshly ground pepper

Heat oil in large saucepan or skillet. Add green pepper, onion, and garlic and sauté until tender. Add tomatoes, water, tomato paste, parsley, **BUTTER BUDS**®, basil, thyme, and pepper. Mix well. Simmer, covered, 25 to 30 minutes, stirring frequently.

About 4 cups

PER SERVING (½ cup:) Calories: 70 Protein: 2gm
Carbohydrate: 10gm   Fat: 2gm   Sodium: 140mg

Note: By using **BUTTER BUDS**® instead of vegetable oil in this recipe, you have saved 114 calories per serving.

Gnocchi

1 package **BETTY CROCKER**® Hash Brown Potatoes
2¼ cups boiling water
1 teaspoon salt
¼ cup milk
1 tablespoon margarine or butter
Dash of pepper
¼ cup margarine or butter
1 cup grated Parmesan cheese

Grease rectangular pan, 13x9x2 inches. Mix potatoes, water, and salt in 2-quart saucepan. Cook over medium-high heat, stirring constantly, until thickened, about 5 minutes (spoon will stand upright in mixture); remove from heat. Stir in milk and 1 tablespoon margarine thoroughly; spread in pan. Cool; cover and refrigerate until firm, 2 to 3 hours.

Heat oven to 350°. Cut mixture into 1½-inch squares or circles. (Dip knife in cold water to prevent sticking.) Place cakes, overlapping, in ungreased rectangular baking dish, 12x7½x2 inches. Dot with ¼ cup margarine; sprinkle with cheese. Bake uncovered until crisp and golden, about 30 minutes. *6 servings*

HIGH ALTITUDE DIRECTIONS (3500 to 6500 feet): Cook potato-water mixture about 9 minutes. Continue as directed except—increase bake time to 40 to 45 minutes.

Ricotta Gnocchi

3 lb. **PRECIOUS® Ricotta**
2 lb. flour
2 Tbsp. olive oil
3 eggs
Pinch of salt

Mix **PRECIOUS® Ricotta** and flour. Make a well, drop in eggs, oil, salt, and knead. Handle as little as possible. Let dough rest for 5 minutes. Roll dough into long rope-like strips about ¾ inch thick. Cut into ¾ inch pieces. Use fork prongs to make a dented design on each piece. Drop into 4 quarts of rapidly boiling salted water for 8 minutes. Drain and serve with favorite sauce.

Ricotta Cavatelli or Gnocchi

4 cups all-purpose flour
Salt
1 container (15 ounces) **POLLY-O® Ricotta**
2 8-ounce cans tomato sauce
POLLY-O® Grated Parmesan or **Romano Cheese**

Combine flour, pinch of salt, and ricotta; mix thoroughly. Knead on lightly floured board until dough is smooth. Set dough aside on one corner of floured board. Cut small pieces from dough, roll quickly into finger thin rolls (about ½-inch in diameter) and cut into pieces ½-inch long. Flatten each piece gently, and bring long sides together to form hollow tube. Arrange separately on a floured board or cloth and sprinkle with flour. Drop gently into rapidly boiling salted water. Cook 12 to 15 minutes, stirring occasionally to prevent sticking. Remove from water with strainer, drain well and serve with tomato sauce and a generous sprinkling of grated cheese.

6 servings

Ravioli Pepperonata

2 medium-sized eggplants
1 tablespoon salt
¼ cup chopped green pepper
¼ cup chopped red pepper
¼ cup onions
¼ cup cooking oil
2 cans (15 oz. each) **CHEF BOY-AR-DEE® Beef Ravioli in Tomato Sauce**
6 pitted black olives, sliced
¼ cup grated Parmesan cheese

Cut eggplant in half lengthwise. Scoop out eggplant pulp with a large spoon or melon-baller. Salt pulp and allow to stand for 15 minutes to remove excess water. Dry with absorbent towel. Blanch eggplant shells for five minutes in boiling water; drain. Sauté pepper, onion and eggplant pulp in oil until soft, but not brown. Add Beef Ravioli in Tomato Sauce, sliced olives and cheese. Fill blanched shells with Beef Ravioli mixture. Cover tops with aluminum foil. Bake in 350°F oven for 20 minutes.

Serves 4

Frigo Ravioli

Raviolis:
4 eggs
6 cups sifted flour
¾ cup water
2 Tbsp. oil

Put flour in bowl. Make a well and add oil and eggs. Work in enough water to make a good dough. Put on floured board and knead until smooth. Cover and let rest for 30 minutes.

Ravioli Filling:
3 lb. **FRIGO Ricotta Cheese**
6 eggs
2 Tbsp. chopped parsley
½ cup **FRIGO Grated Parmesan Cheese**
1½ tsp. salt
¼ tsp. pepper
1 cup (4 oz.) **FRIGO Shredded Mozzarella Cheese**

Roll small amount of dough into thin strips, 2½ inches wide and 3 inches long. Fill with filling on one half and fold over remaining dough. Seal edges together with fork dipped in flour. Cook in salted boiling water (add 1 Tbsp. of oil to prevent sticking). Serve with **FRIGO Grated Parmesan Cheese**. For SAUCE, use the **FRIGO** Basic Tomato Pasta Sauce*. *Serves 12*

Note: Ravioli can be frozen for future use.

*Frigo Basic Tomato Pasta Sauce

1 medium size onion, chopped
⅔ cup butter
⅓ cup olive oil
1 12 oz. can tomato paste
1 2 pound can whole peeled tomatoes, drained
2 15 oz. cans tomato sauce
1 Tbsp. salt
1 Tbsp. pepper
⅛ tsp. garlic powder
¼ cup **FRIGO Grated Parmesan Cheese**
Herb bag**

Brown onion in butter over low heat. Add olive oil and remaining ingredients.

Simmer sauce about 2 hours over very low heat. Remove herb bag before mixing with pasta. Sauce is enough for one pound of spaghetti, lasagne, rigatoni, or manicotti.

**Herb Bag: Cut a 3 by 4 inch piece of cheesecloth or other porous cloth. Place the following herbs on the cloth, then tie with string and put it in the sauce.
2 tsp. rosemary
1½ tsp. basil
1½ tsp. oregano

COOKIN' GOOD™
GRADE A CHICKEN

Cookin' Good™ Tetrazzini

1 clove of garlic crushed
½ cup chopped onion
¼ cup butter or margarine
⅓ cup flour
1 14½-oz. can of chicken broth or 1⅔ cups of homemade chicken stock
½ teaspoon salt
¼ teaspoon pepper
¼ cup light cream
¼ cup sherry
2 tablespoons of chopped pimentos (1 2-ounce jar)
½ cup sliced black olives
2 cups of cooked cubed **COOKIN' GOOD™ Chicken**
1 8-ounce package of spaghetti broken into 3 inch pieces cooked in salted water 5 minutes
5 ounce package of grated Parmesan cheese (reserve 2 tablespoons)
2 dashes of nutmeg
Paprika

In a large saucepan, sauté onion in melted margarine or butter. Add garlic and continue to sauté until tender. Remove from range and stir in flour, salt and pepper. Cook 2-3 minutes stirring constantly. Gradually blend in cream, sherry, and broth, stirring after each addition. Cook over medium heat, stirring constantly until thickened. Add chicken and remaining ingredients to sauce. Toss well. Pour mixture into a greased 2½ quart casserole. Sprinkle with paprika and cheese. BAKE casserole at 350° 25-30 minutes or MICROWAVE 12-15 minutes. May be halved and frozen for a future meal.   *Serves 6*

Mueller's®

Mueller's® Chicken Tetrazzini

1 can (4 ounces) sliced mushrooms, drained, reserving liquid
⅓ cup chopped onion
4 tablespoons butter or margarine
3 tablespoons flour
1½ cups chicken broth
½ cup light cream
½ teaspoon salt
Dash pepper
½ cup dry vermouth or chicken broth
¾ cup grated Parmesan cheese
8 ounces **MUELLER'S® Thin Spaghetti**
2 cups diced cooked chicken

In saucepan, cook mushrooms and onion in butter until soft; stir in flour. Gradually add 1½ cups broth, cream and reserved mushroom liquid; cook, stirring, until sauce thickens. Remove from heat. Add salt, pepper, vermouth and ¼ cup of the cheese; set aside. Meanwhile, cook spaghetti as directed on package; drain. Combine spaghetti and chicken in 2-quart casserole; pour sauce over and mix lightly. Sprinkle with remaining cheese. Bake at 375°F. for 20 minutes or until bubbling.   *4 to 6 servings*

San Giorgio®

Rotini Tetrazzini

6 tablespoons butter
6 tablespoons unsifted all-purpose flour
1¾ cups chicken broth
½ cup heavy cream
2 egg yolks, slightly beaten
2 cups cooked chicken, cubed
1 cup sautéed mushrooms
¼ cup chopped pimentos
¼ cup chopped fresh parsley
¼ cup dry white wine
Salt and pepper to taste
2 tablespoons grated Parmesan cheese
½ package (8 ounces) **SAN GIORGIO® Rotini**

Melt butter; stir in flour. Gradually add chicken broth and heavy cream. Cook and stir constantly over medium heat until mixture begins to boil; boil and stir 1 minute. Remove from heat. Add small amount of sauce to egg yolks; blend well. Return egg mixture to sauce; stir until smooth. Add chicken, mushrooms, pimentos, parsley, wine, salt and pepper to sauce; keep warm over low heat. Cook Rotini according to package directions; drain. Toss immediately with sauce mixture; top with Parmesan cheese.
4 to 6 servings

South African Rock Lobster Tetrazzini

1 lb. of frozen **SOUTH AFRICAN ROCK LOBSTER Tails**
¼ cup butter
¼ cup flour
2 cups canned chicken broth
2 egg yolks
2 tablespoons sherry
⅓ cup light cream
1 pkg. (10 oz.) frozen asparagus spears, cooked and drained
1 pkg. (8 oz.) spaghetti, cooked and drained
2 tablespoons grated Parmesan cheese
¼ cup slivered blanched almonds

Drop frozen **SOUTH AFRICAN ROCK LOBSTER Tails** into salted boiling water. When water reboils, cook tails for 2 to 3 minutes. Drain immediately and drench with cold water. Cut away underside membrane with kitchen shears. Remove meat and dice. Melt butter and stir in flour. Gradually stir in chicken broth. Cook over low heat, stirring constantly until mixture bubbles and thickens. Beat egg yolks, sherry and cream together. Beat hot sauce into egg mixture. Reheat while stirring until mixture just bubbles. Fold in rock lobster meat. Put asparagus spears into 6 individual casseroles. Top with cooked spaghetti. Spoon hot rock lobster mixture over spaghetti. Sprinkle top with Parmesan cheese and almonds. Put casseroles under broiler and broil until cheese and almonds are golden.   *Yield: 6 servings*

Favorite recipe from **South African Rock Lobster Service Corp.**

Turkey Tetrazzini

6 slices roasted **BUTTERBALL® SWIFT'S PREMIUM®** Turkey
½ stick (¼ cup) butter
⅔ cup sliced onion
¼ cup flour
1 teaspoon salt
¼ teaspoon white pepper
½ teaspoon poultry seasoning
¼ teaspoon dry mustard
2 cups milk
⅔ cup shredded sharp Cheddar cheese
2 tablespoons chopped pimiento
2 tablespoons sherry
4-ounce can mushrooms, stems and pieces, undrained
7-ounce package spaghetti, cooked, drained
⅓ cup shredded sharp Cheddar cheese

Melt butter in saucepan. Sauté onion in butter until tender. Blend in flour and seasonings. Remove from heat. Gradually add milk. Stirring constantly, cook until mixture thickens. Add ⅔ cup cheese and pimiento, stirring until cheese melts. Add sherry and mushrooms and liquid to cheese sauce. Place a layer of spaghetti in a 12 x 7½ inch (2 quart) casserole. Cover with a layer of turkey and a layer of sauce. Repeat, finishing with a layer of sauce. Sprinkle ⅓ cup cheese over top. Bake in a 400°F oven about 25 minutes.

Yield: 6 servings

Note: Casserole may be assembled in advance and frozen. To serve, heat, covered, in a 350°F oven for 1½ hours or until hot.

Lasagne

Hamburger Helper®

Easy Lasagne

1 pound ground beef
½ cup chopped onion
1 clove garlic, finely chopped
1 package **BETTY CROCKER® HAMBURGER HELPER®** Mix for Lasagne
2 cups hot water
1 can (16 ounces) whole tomatoes
1½ cups dry cottage cheese (small curd)
1 cup shredded mozzarella cheese (about 4 ounces)

Cook and stir ground beef, onion and garlic in 10-inch skillet until beef is brown; drain. Stir in Macaroni, Sauce Mix, water and tomatoes (with liquid); break up tomatoes with fork. Heat to boiling, stirring constantly; reduce heat. Cover and simmer, stirring occasionally, 15 to 20 minutes. Stir in cottage cheese; sprinkle with mozzarella cheese. Cover and cook over low heat until cheese is melted, 2 to 3 minutes.

6 to 8 servings

HIGH ALTITUDE DIRECTIONS (3500 to 6500 feet): Increase hot water to 2½ cups and simmer time to 25 to 30 minutes.

REDPACK

Lasagne

2 pounds ground chuck
2 cloves garlic, minced
3 large onions, chopped
1 tablespoon oil
1 tablespoon Italian Herbs*
¼ cup butter
1 tablespoon salt
¼ teaspoon pepper
¼ cup flour
1 cup hot water
1 cup red wine
1 can (16 ounce) **REDPACK Tomato Puree**
1 can (28 ounce) **REDPACK Whole Tomatoes in Juice**
1 package (16 ounce) lasagne noodles
4 cups grated Monterey Jack cheese
1 container (16 ounce) ricotta cheese**

Brown meat, garlic and onions in oil. Sprinkle with 2 teaspoons Italian Herbs. Remove from pan. Melt butter, add salt, pepper and remaining Herbs; stir in flour. Add water, wine, tomato puree and liquid from whole tomatoes. Cook, stirring until sauce thickens. Break up tomatoes; add to sauce with juice. To bake, use two pans, (11¾x7½x1¾-inch) or 1 pan (18 x 12 x 2-inch). Pour sauce to cover bottom of pan(s). Arrange uncooked lasagne noodles to fit pan. Cover lasagne with more sauce. Add layer of meat mixture, grated cheese and ricotta. End with top layer of lasagne. Cover with remaining sauce and top with grated cheese. Bake covered at 375 degrees F. for 45 minutes. Uncover and continue baking 20 minutes. Let stand before serving. Garnish with chopped parsley, if desired.

Serves 15

*Available in grocery store spice section.
**Small curd cottage cheese may be substituted.

Wheat Germ Beef Lasagna

2 Tbsp. cooking oil
½ cup finely chopped onion
1 clove garlic, minced
1 lb. lean ground beef
2 tsp. salt
½ tsp. oregano leaves, crushed
¼ tsp. basil leaves, crushed
¼ tsp. pepper
2 cans (6 oz. each) tomato paste
1¾ cups water
8 oz. lasagna noodles
12 oz. sliced mozzarella cheese
2 cups (16 oz.) ricotta cheese
¾ cup **KRETSCHMER Regular Wheat Germ**
¼ cup grated Parmesan cheese

Sauté . . . . onion and garlic in oil until onion is tender.
Add . . . . beef and salt to onion mixture. Cook over medium heat until meat is browned. Drain off fat.
Stir in . . . . oregano, basil, pepper, tomato paste and water. Cover and simmer 15 minutes.
Cook . . . . lasagna noodles as package directs. Drain and rinse in cold water.
Cover . . . . bottom of 13 x 9 x 2-inch pan with ⅓ of the noodles.

Arrange ...... ⅓ of the mozzarella cheese on noodles. Dot with
⅓ of the ricotta cheese.
Spread ...... with ⅓ of the meat sauce. Sprinkle with ¼ cup
wheat germ.
Repeat ...... layers two more times.
Sprinkle ..... with Parmesan cheese. Cover.
Bake........ at 350° for 45 minutes until thoroughly heated.
Let stand ..... 10 minutes before cutting and serving.

Makes 8-10 servings

Vegetable Lasagne

1 pkg. (8-oz.) Lasagne noodles
2 cups (8-oz.) **DARIGOLD Mozzarella Cheese**, grated
2 cups (1 pint) **DARI-LITE 1% Cottage Cheese**
2 **DARIGOLD Eggs**
1 pkg. (9-oz.) frozen Italian-Style green beans, partly
thawed
2 cups fresh carrots, sliced and blanched
¾ pound fresh sliced zucchini
4 cups spaghetti sauce
⅔ cup grated Parmesan Cheese

Cook noodles as package directs; drain. Rinse with cold water and
set aside. In medium bowl, mix Mozzarella Cheese, Cottage
Cheese and eggs. In large bowl, mix green beans, carrots, zucchini and sauce. Spread ¼ of the vegetable mixture over bottom of
buttered 13x9-inch baking dish. Arrange ⅓ of the noodles across
the sauce. Top with ⅓ of cheese mixture. Repeat layering, ending
with vegetable mixture. Sprinkle with Parmesan cheese. Bake in a
preheated 375 degree oven for 25 minutes. Let stand 5 minutes
before serving. *Makes 8-10 servings*

Calories: Approximately 266 calories per serving.

Lasagne Roll-Ups

4 quarts water
4 teaspoons salt
1 tablespoon oil
8 pieces **AMERICAN BEAUTY® Lasagne**
1 quart prepared spaghetti sauce
1 lb. Italian sausage or ground beef
¼ cup chopped onion
½ cup dry bread crumbs
1 teaspoon salt
½ teaspoon basil leaves
¼ teaspoon pepper
2 cups (8 oz.) shredded mozzarella cheese
12-oz. carton cottage cheese
1 egg, beaten
Grated Parmesan cheese, if desired

Heat oven to 350°F. Boil water in large deep pot with 4 teaspoons
salt and oil (to prevent boiling over). Add lasagne; stir. Cook
uncovered after water returns to a full rolling boil for 10 to 12
minutes. Stir occasionally. Drain and rinse under cold water.

Spread 2 cups of spaghetti sauce over bottom of 13 x 9-inch
baking dish. In large skillet, brown sausage with onion over
medium heat; drain. Add bread crumbs, 1 teaspoon salt, basil,
pepper, mozzarella cheese, cottage cheese and egg. Cut each

lasagne noodle in half crosswise; spread about 3 tablespoons of
sausage mixture evenly on each half. Roll up from shorter side and
place seam down in pan. Pour remaining sauce over top.

Cover and bake at 350°F. for 1 hour. Serve rolls with sauce.
Serve with Parmesan cheese, if desired. *8 servings*

HIGH ALTITUDE—Above 3500 Feet: Cooking times may need to be
increased slightly for lasagne; no additional changes.

NUTRITIONAL INFORMATION PER SERVING
SERVING SIZE: ⅛ of recipe

		PERCENT U.S. RDA PER SERVING	
Calories	536		
Protein	25 g	Protein	39
Carbohydrate	37 g	Vitamin A	6
Fat	32 g	Vitamin C	—
Sodium	1429 mg	Thiamine	22
Potassium	113 mg	Riboflavin	30
		Niacin	13
		Calcium	32
		Iron	20

Neapolitan Lasagne

1 lb. **LA ROSA® Lasagne**

Sauce:
1 small onion, diced
1 clove garlic
¼ cup olive oil
1-1 lb. 14 oz. can tomatoes
1 tablespoon chopped parsley
3 basil leaves
1 can tomato paste
Salt and pepper to taste

Meatballs:
½ lb. chopped round steak
¼ cup **LA ROSA® Bread Crumbs**
⅛ cup milk
1 egg, beaten
3 tablespoons **LA ROSA® Grated Cheese**
2 tablespoons chopped parsley
Salt and pepper to taste

Filling:
1 pound Ricotta cheese or cottage cheese
1-8 oz. mozzarella cheese, sliced
3 Tbsp. **LA ROSA® Grated Cheese**

Prepare sauce by browning ingredients in saucepan, and simmer
for 15 minutes. Prepare meatballs by combining meat, egg, milk,
cheese and salt and pepper in a mixing bowl. Add parsley and
bread crumbs, mixing thoroughly. Shape meatballs and brown in
olive oil. Add meatballs to sauce and simmer 30 minutes. While
sauce is simmering, boil 6 quarts of water. Add 3 tablespoons of
salt. When boiling rapidly, slowly add Lasagne and cook for 15
minutes. Drain well and rinse in cold water. Before arranging
casserole, separate meatballs from sauce. Crush meatballs to allow
for proper spreading between layers. Arrange 13 x 9¼ x 2 casserole with several spoonsful of sauce on bottom, then a layer of
Lasagne and then several slices of mozzarella cheese. Next add 4
or 5 tablespoons of ricotta or cottage cheese, sprinkle with grated
cheese. Finally, spread ¼ of sauce and ¼ of crushed meatballs.
Repeat, until all the Lasagne is used ending with a layer of
Lasagne, sauce, and top with grated cheese. Bake 20 minutes in
moderate (350°F.) oven.

Beef Lasagna

- 1 8-ounce package **HEALTH VALLEY® Whole Wheat Lasagna Pasta**
- 2 tablespoons **HEALTH VALLEY® BEST BLEND Oil**
- 1 clove garlic, minced
- ¼ cup chopped green onions
- ¼ cup chopped celery
- ¼ cup chopped green peppers
- ¼ cup chopped sweet, red peppers
- ¾ cup sliced mushrooms
- ¼ cup chopped parsley
- 1 1-pound package **HEALTH VALLEY® Ground Beef,** thawed and drained
- 2 15-ounce cans **HEALTH VALLEY® Tomato Sauce**
- 1 teaspoon natural soy sauce (Tamari)
- ½ teaspoon oregano
- ½ teaspoon basil
- 1 12-ounce package **HEALTH VALLEY® Raw Milk Colby Cheese,** thinly sliced
- 1 cup (⅓ package) shredded **HEALTH VALLEY® Raw Milk Sharp Cheddar Cheese**

Preheat oven to 350°F. and oil a 10 x 6 x 2-inch baking dish. Cook pasta according to package directions. Do not drain, but allow to cool slightly while preparing sauce.

In a large skillet, heat oil and sauté garlic, onions, celery, green and red peppers, mushrooms and parsley. Remove from skillet and set aside. Add beef to skillet and cook, turning constantly, until meat is lightly browned. Pour off fat, then add 1 can of tomato sauce, soy sauce, oregano and basil. Simmer for about 5 minutes, then add vegetables.

Cover the bottom of the baking dish with a thin layer of sauce from the remaining can of tomato sauce, then layer into pan; pasta, half of meat sauce, half of cheese slices and a thin layer of plain tomato sauce. Make a second layer; pasta, second half of meat sauce, remaining half of cheese slices and thin layer of plain sauce. Then add to the top layer; pasta, shredded cheese and layer of plain sauce. Bake in preheated oven for 45 minutes until cheese is melted and sauce is bubbly. Total Preparation Time: 1¼ hours.

Italian-Chef Lasagne Imbottite

- 1 lb. lasagne
- 2 cups **PASTORELLI® Italian-Chef Spaghetti Sauce**
- ½ cup **PASTORELLI® Italian-Chef Pizza Sauce**
- 1 lb. fresh ricotta (Italian Cottage Cheese) or dry baker's cottage cheese
- ¾ lb. mozzarella cheese
- ½ lb. ground beef or Italian style sausage (browned)
- ½ cup grated Parmesan cheese

Cook one pound lasagne in rapidly boiling salted water until tender, al dente, not soft; drain.

Spread three tablespoons **PASTORELLI® Italian-Chef Sauces** on medium baking pan. Put one layer of lasagne noodles over this. Spread sauce, sliced mozzarella cheese mixed with browned meat, put layer of ricotta cheese on top, sprinkle with Parmesan cheese. Repeat with another layer of noodles etc. until all ingredients have been layered and used.

Bake in moderate oven for about 15 minutes. Cut in squares. Serve hot. *A complete dinner serving 6 to 8 people*

Sausage Lasagna

- 1 pound **RATH® BLACK HAWK Sausage**
- ¾ cup chopped onion
- ½ teaspoon garlic powder
- 3½ cups tomatoes (1 lb.-12 oz. can)
- ¾ cup tomato paste (6 oz. can)
- 2¼ teaspoons salt
- 1 teaspoon oregano
- 1 large (12 oz.) or 2 small (6 oz.) packages lasagna noodles or other broad noodles
- 1 cup small-curd cottage cheese (8 oz.)
- 2 cups coarsely shredded Cheddar cheese (about 8 oz.)
- ¾ cup grated Parmesan cheese (3 oz.)

Brown sausage. Drain. Add onion and garlic powder and cook until tender. Mash tomatoes and add tomato paste, salt, oregano. Add to **RATH® BLACK HAWK Sausage** and onion mixture. Simmer for 15 minutes. Cook lasagna noodles in boiling, salted water until tender. Rinse lasagna noodles with cool water until noodles are cool enough to handle. Drain. Lightly grease a 9 x 13 inch pan. Arrange ⅓ of noodles in pan, cover with ⅓ each of tomato meat sauce, cottage cheese, Cheddar cheese and Parmesan cheese. Repeat layers twice ending with cheeses on top. Bake in moderate oven (350 degrees F.) about 40 minutes, or until surface is browned and bubbly. Serve at once. *Makes 6 servings*

Note: This is especially good warmed over so can be made ahead.

Mushroom Lasagna

- 3 cans (3 oz.) **BinB® Broiled in Butter Sliced Mushrooms,** drained—reserving broth
- 1 package (16 oz.) lasagna noodles
- 1 package (8 oz.) cream cheese, softened
- 3 cups cottage cheese
- 1 tablespoon parsley flakes
- ½ teaspoon salt
- ½ teaspoon basil
- ¼ teaspoon oregano
- ⅛ teaspoon garlic powder
- 1 can (15 oz.) tomato sauce
- ¾ cup grated Parmesan cheese

Drain mushrooms, reserving buttery broth. Combine cream cheese, cottage cheese, salt, garlic powder and parsley. Set aside. Combine buttery broth, oregano, basil and tomato sauce and simmer about 10 minutes. Layer noodles and cheese mixture in buttered 9 inch × 13 inch shallow baking dish. Sprinkle each layer with 1 can of mushroom slices, tomato sauce and ¼ cup Parmesan cheese. Bake, uncovered, in preheated 350°F. oven for 30 minutes. Uncover and continue for 15 minutes.

Makes 8 to 10 servings

Almond Zucchini Lasagna

½ pound lean ground beef
¾ cup chopped onion
1 clove garlic, minced or pressed
1 can (15 ounces) tomato sauce
1 can (6 ounces) tomato paste
2 teaspoons Italian herb seasoning, crushed
½ teaspoon sugar
¼ teaspoon pepper
1 carton (8 ounces) creamed cottage cheese
¾ cup **BLUE DIAMOND® Blanched Slivered Almonds**, toasted
1 egg, lightly beaten
4 medium zucchini
2 tablespoons flour
1 cup shredded mozzarella cheese

In medium skillet, cook beef, onion and garlic until meat is browned. Drain. Stir in tomato sauce, tomato paste, Italian seasoning, sugar and pepper. Simmer 20 minutes, stirring occasionally. Combine cottage cheese, ½ cup of the almonds and egg. Slice zucchini lengthwise ¼-inch thick. In bottom of 12 x 8-inch baking dish, arrange half of zucchini. Sprinkle with 1 tablespoon of the flour. Spread cottage cheese mixture, then half of meat mixture on top. Repeat with remaining zucchini, flour and meat mixture. Bake at 350° F., 30 to 40 minutes, or until zucchini is tender. Sprinkle with cheese and remaining ¼ cup almonds. Let stand 10 minutes. *Makes 6 to 8 servings*

Contadina® Lasagna Roll-Ups

1 pound sweet Italian sausage
½ cup chopped onion
1 crushed garlic clove
1⅓ cups (two 6-ounce cans) **CONTADINA® Tomato Paste**
1⅔ cups water
1 teaspoon oregano leaves
½ teaspoon basil leaves
⅔ cup (10-ounce package) cooked, thoroughly drained, frozen chopped spinach
2 cups (1 pint) ricotta cheese
1 cup grated Parmesan cheese
1½ cups (6 ounces) shredded mozzarella cheese
1 slightly beaten egg
½ teaspoon salt
¼ teaspoon pepper
8 cooked, drained lasagna noodles

Remove casings from sausage; crumble. Brown sausage with onion and garlic in saucepan. Pour off excess fat. Add tomato paste, water, oregano, and basil. Cover; boil gently 20 minutes. Combine spinach, ricotta cheese, Parmesan cheese, *1 cup mozzarella cheese*, egg, salt, and pepper in medium bowl. Mix thoroughly. Spread about ½ cup mixture on each noodle. Roll up. Place seam-side down in 12 x 7½ x 2-inch baking dish. Pour sauce over rolls. Top with *remaining ½ cup mozzarella cheese*. Bake in moderate oven (350° F.) 30-40 minutes, or until heated through. *Makes 6 to 8 servings*

RAGÚ

Homestyle Canneloni Classico

1½ pounds ground beef
1 small onion, chopped
1 package (10 oz.) frozen chopped spinach, cooked and squeezed dry
1½ cups (6 oz.) shredded mozzarella cheese, divided
½ cup bread crumbs
1 egg, slightly beaten
¼ cup grated Parmesan cheese, divided
1 teaspoon oregano
½ teaspoon salt
¼ teaspoon black pepper
1 jar (15½ oz.) **RAGÚ® Homestyle Spaghetti Sauce**, any flavor
½ pound (about 8) lasagna noodles, cooked and drained

Preheat oven to 350°F. In large skillet, brown beef; add onion and sauté until translucent. Pour off fat. Add spinach, 1 cup mozzarella, bread crumbs, egg, ½ cheese and seasonings. Mix well; set aside. In 11 x 7-inch baking dish, spread 1 cup **Homestyle Spaghetti Sauce.** Cut each lasagna noodle in half crosswise. Place quarter cup of filling on each noodle half; roll and place seam-side down in baking dish. Pour remaining sauce over canneloni; sprinkle with remaining cheeses. Cover tightly with foil; bake 30 minutes. Uncover, bake 5 minutes more. *Serves 8*

Macaroni

Quick Macaroni Parmesan

1 (7 ounce) package elbow macaroni
¼ cup butter, softened
½ cup instant nonfat dry milk
⅓ cup water
½ teaspoon salt
2 cups shredded sharp Cheddar cheese
¼ cup grated Parmesan cheese

Cook macaroni according to package directions. Drain. Add butter and toss until melted. Return to low heat. Blend nonfat dry milk with water and salt. Pour over macaroni; add Cheddar cheese. Stir until cheese is melted. If desired; add any of the variations listed below. Turn into heated serving dish; sprinkle with Parmesan cheese.

VARIATIONS:

1. 8 ounces (2 cups) fully cooked ham, cubed and 1 (4 ounce) can sliced mushrooms, drained.
2. 1 (6½ ounce) can tuna, drained and flaked and ¼ cup sliced olives.
3. 1 (12 ounce) can luncheon meat, cut in cubes and 2 tablespoons chopped chives.
4. 4 frankfurters, sliced and ¼ cup chopped green pepper.
Yield 3 to 4 servings

Favorite recipe from **American Dry Milk Institute, Inc.**

Cheese Casserole

½ lb. macaroni twirls
1 pkg. American cheese
1 can **ROKEACH** Tomato-Mushroom Sauce

Boil macaroni until soft. Then place one layer of macaroni in a baking dish, add layer of American cheese. Keep alternating layers of macaroni and cheese. Then top with **ROKEACH'S Tomato-Mushroom Sauce** making sure it seeps throughout the dish. Bake at 375° for 15-20 minutes.

Homestyle Pasta Bake

1 pound ziti or elbow macaroni
1 egg
1 pound cottage cheese
½ teaspoon **FRENCH'S® Italian Seasoning**
½ pound Italian sausage*
1 envelope (1¾-oz.) **FRENCH'S® Thick, Homemade Style Spaghetti Sauce Mix**
2 cans (6-oz.each) tomato paste
2½ cups water
1½ cups shredded mozzarella cheese

Cook and drain macaroni. Lightly beat egg in large mixing bowl; stir in cottage cheese, Italian seasoning, and the cooked macaroni. Spoon into greased 13 x 9-inch baking dish. Cover loosely with foil. Bake at 350° for 30 minutes. Meanwhile, cut sausage in 1-inch pieces and brown in large saucepan, stirring frequently. Add sauce mix, tomato paste, and water. Cover and simmer 15 to 20 minutes, stirring occasionally. Spoon about half the sauce on top of macaroni; sprinkle with mozzarella cheese. Bake, uncovered, 10 to 15 minutes. Cut in squares and serve with remaining sausage and sauce.   *8 to 10 servings*

*If preferred, omit sausage. Brown 1 pound ground beef and add to spaghetti sauce.

Slim Herb Mac and Cheese

1 (7 oz.) package or 2 cups uncooked **CREAMETTES® Elbow Macaroni**, cooked as package directs and drained
¼ cup low calorie margarine
¼ cup unsifted flour
1 teaspoon dry mustard
1 teaspoon garlic salt
¼ to ½ teaspoon basil leaves
½ teaspoon paprika
2 cups skim milk
8 slices low calorie cheese cut into small pieces
2 teaspoons corn flake crumbs
Chopped parsley

Preheat oven to 350. In small saucepan, over low heat, melt margarine; stir in flour, mustard, salt, basil and paprika. Gradually stir in milk; cook and stir until thickened. Add cheese product; cook and stir until melted. Remove from heat; stir in cooked macaroni. Turn into 1½ quart baking dish; top with crumbs. Bake 20 minutes or until bubbly. Garnish with parsley. Refrigerate leftovers.   *Makes 8 servings*

Macaroni & Beans Italiano

½ cup chopped onion
½ cup chopped green pepper
1 medium zucchini, cut into ⅛-inch slices
3 tablespoons margarine or olive oil
¾ cup **HEINZ** Tomato Ketchup
¾ cup water
1 teaspoon salt
½ teaspoon oregano leaves
¼ teaspoon garlic salt
⅛ teaspoon pepper
1 can (1 pound) **HEINZ** Vegetarian Beans in Tomato Sauce
1½ cups cooked macaroni
Grated Parmesan cheese

Sauté first 3 ingredients in margarine until tender. Stir in ketchup and next 5 ingredients. Combine with beans and macaroni in a 1½-quart casserole. Bake in 375°F. oven, 35-40 minutes. Stir occasionally. Serve with Parmesan cheese.

Makes 4-5 servings (about 4½ cups)

MICROWAVE METHOD:
Power Level—HIGH. Omit margarine. Decrease salt to ½ teaspoon and pepper to dash. Place onion, green pepper and zucchini in a 1½-quart casserole. Cover casserole with plastic film, turning one edge back slightly to vent. Microwave 6 minutes or until vegetables are tender. Stir in ketchup and remaining ingredients except Parmesan cheese. Cover; microwave 5 minutes, stirring once. Stir and let stand, covered, 5 minutes. Serve with Parmesan cheese.

Pasta ala Potenza

1 pound rotelle macaroni
4 tablespoons butter
1 cup chopped fresh mushrooms
2 tablespoons flour
1½ cups milk
½ teaspoon salt
1 cup shredded mozzarella cheese
1 6-ounce jar **GOLD'S White Horseradish**, drained

Cook macaroni until al dente. Drain well. Meanwhile make mushroom sauce. In a saucepan, heat butter and sauté mushrooms until limp. Stir in flour and continue to cook, stirring constantly, about 2 minutes. Beat in milk. Season with salt. Cook, stirring, until thickened. Add mushroom sauce and cheese to macaroni. Toss.

Place mixture in 3-quart casserole. Sprinkle horseradish on top, then spread over top with tines of fork. Bake in preheated 350-degree oven for 20 to 25 minutes until top is browned.

Linguine

Classic Linguine with Clams

1 can (10 oz.) **BUMBLE BEE® Whole Baby Clams**
1 medium onion, minced
2 large cloves garlic, pressed
¼ cup olive oil
2 tablespoons butter
¼ cup dry white wine
¼ cup minced parsley
¼ teaspoon black pepper
6 ounces cooked linguine

Drain clams, reserving liquid. In medium skillet, sauté onion and garlic in oil and butter. Stir in wine and clam liquid; boil about 3 minutes to reduce liquid. Stir in clams, parsley and pepper. Heat thoroughly. Serve over cooked pasta.

Makes 2 generous servings

Linguine with Parsley Pesto Sauce

1 pound **FOULDS' Linguine** or **Spaghetti**
Salt
4-6 quarts boiling water
1 cup parsley sprigs
½ cup pine nuts
2 cloves garlic
1 tablespoon dried basil
½ cup olive or salad oil
¼ cup water
½ cup grated Parmesan cheese
Dash pepper

Gradually add linguine and 2 tablespoons salt to rapidly boiling water so that water continues to boil. Cook uncovered, stirring occasionally, until tender. Drain in colander.

While linguine is cooking, combine parsley, nuts, garlic, basil, oil and water in electric blender container. Blend until smooth. Gradually add cheese until well mixed. Season to taste with salt and pepper. Toss linguine with sauce and serve immediately.

CONVENTIONAL METHOD: *Makes 8 servings*
Finely chop parsley and nuts; crush garlic. Thoroughly mix together with remaining ingredients in serving bowl.

Port Clyde Foods, Inc.

Pasta con Pesce

6 medium size ripe tomatoes
2 tablespoons chopped parsley
1 teaspoon dried basil, crumbled
3 tablespoons lemon juice
3 tablespoons vegetable oil
1 teaspoon finely chopped garlic
½ teaspoon salt
¼ teaspoon pepper
3 cans (3¾ oz.) **PORT CLYDE** or **HOLMES Fish Steaks,** drained (oil, mustard or tomato flavor)
1 pound linguini or spaghetti
1 tablespoon soft butter

Dip tomatoes in boiling water until skin comes off easily, about 15 seconds. Peel and chop. Combine with parsley, basil, lemon juice, oil, garlic, salt and pepper. Spoon over fish steaks in shallow bowl; reserve, keeping warm. Cook pasta in boiling salted water, following package label directions; drain, return to kettle and toss with butter. Stir in about one-third of sauce. Divide among six heated deep plates. Top with remaining sauce and serve immediately. Sprinkle with Parmesan cheese, if desired.

Makes 6 servings

DANNON® YOGURT

Pasta with Italian Ham

½ cup grated Parmesan cheese
½ cup **Plain DANNON® Yogurt**
⅓ cup dry white wine
2 tablespoons butter or margarine, melted
1 10-ounce package frozen asparagus spears, cooked and drained
4 ounces thinly sliced prosciutto or very thinly sliced smoked ham, cut in 1-inch strips
8 ounces linguini, fettucine, spaghetti or other pasta
Grated Parmesan cheese, optional

Combine ½ cup Parmesan cheese, yogurt, wine and butter in small bowl. Stir in asparagus and prosciutto; set aside. Prepare pasta according to package directions. Drain well. Place pasta on warm serving platter; toss with cheese mixture. Sprinkle with additional Parmesan cheese, if desired. Serve immediately. *Serves 6*

B and B LIQUEUR

Linguine with Clam Sauce

2 tablespoons margarine or butter
1 tablespoon peanut oil
3 cloves garlic, finely minced
¼ cup half and half
¼ cup **B&B® Liqueur**
2 cans (6½ oz. each) chopped clams, drained
¼ teaspoon salt
¼ cup chopped parsley
1 package (8 oz.) linguine, cooked according to package directions

Heat margarine and peanut oil in a skillet over medium heat. Add garlic and sauté 2 minutes, or until tender. Remove skillet from heat; stir in half and half, **B&B® Liqueur,** clams and salt. Return skillet to heat and cook and stir until mixture is heated through. Do not boil. Toss clam sauce and parsley with drained hot linguine and serve. *Makes 4 servings*

Spaghetti

Shrimp Pasta

1 lb. spaghetti, cooked, drained
¼ cup olive oil
2 Tbsp. Parmesan cheese, grated
Pepper, as needed
2 drops **TABASCO®**
¼ cup heavy cream
½ lb. **ATALANTA Frozen Shrimp,** raw, shelled & deveined
3 Tbsp. butter
3 Tbsp. parsley, chopped

Sauté shrimp in butter for 5 minutes. Cut into chunks. Set aside. Heat olive oil and toss in spaghetti, pepper, cheese and **TABASCO®.** Add cream and simmer. Add sautéed shrimp. Sprinkle with parsley and serve. *Yield: 4 servings*

GEISHA®

Red Clam Sauce and Spaghetti

2 10-oz. cans **GEISHA® Brand Whole Baby Clams** and liquid
1 cup minced onions
1 minced clove garlic
2 tablespoons olive oil
1 8-oz. can tomato sauce
1 6-oz. can tomato paste
1 No. 2½ can Italian tomatoes
1 teaspoon salt
⅛ teaspoon pepper
½ teaspoon sweet basil
½ teaspoon oregano
1 tablespoon chopped parsley
1 pound spaghetti (cooked as label directs)
Parmesan cheese (optional)

In Dutch oven sauté onions and garlic in oil until tender. Add tomato sauce, tomato paste, tomatoes, salt, pepper and basil. Cook stirring occasionally until mixture has cooked down about two-thirds and is very thick (about 2 hours). Add clams and their liquid, oregano and parsley. Cook about 10 minutes longer. Serve over hot spaghetti. Sprinkle with cheese if desired.

Makes 4 to 6 servings

Buttery Pasta with Shrimp

3 cups cooked spaghetti (7 oz. uncooked spaghetti)
¾ cup **LAND O LAKES® Sweet Cream Butter**
1 cup (1 med.) chopped green pepper
½ cup (1 small) chopped onion
2 (12 oz.) pkgs. frozen cocktail size (1½ inch) shrimp (not breaded), thawed, drained
1½ tsp. garlic powder
½ tsp. *each* salt and oregano leaves
¼ tsp. pepper
2 cups (2 med.) cubed (½ inch) tomatoes
Grated Parmesan *or* Romano cheese

Have ready cooked spaghetti; set aside. In heavy 3-qt. saucepan melt butter over med. heat (5 to 7 min.). Add remaining ingredients *except* tomatoes and Parmesan cheese; stir to blend. Cook over med. heat (5 to 7 min.). Add cooked spaghetti; stir to blend. Continue cooking over med. heat, stirring occasionally, until spaghetti is heated through (3 to 5 min.). Remove from heat; add tomatoes. Cover; let stand 1 min. or until tomatoes are heated through. To serve, sprinkle with Parmesan cheese.

Yield: 6 (1½ cups) servings

Meatless Spaghetti

1 medium onion, diced
2 stalks of celery, diced
½ green pepper, diced
½ lb. fresh mushrooms, sliced
12 oz. can tomatoes
1 lb. spaghetti, cooked only 8 minutes
4 oz. **CHEEZ-OLA®**, diced
⅛ teaspoon garlic powder
Freshly ground pepper

Brown onion, celery, green pepper and mushrooms in small amount of oil. Add can of tomatoes and cooked spaghetti to oiled 2½ qt. casserole*. Mix in vegetables, diced **CHEEZ-OLA®** and seasonings. Bake at 350 degrees F. for 1½ hours.   *Serves 8*

*May be divided into two small casseroles and one frozen to be used later.

Spaghetti with Garlic and Olives

6 ounces (½ package) **HEALTH VALLEY® Whole Wheat Spaghetti**
½ cup chopped walnuts
½ cup chopped ripe olives
¼ cup chopped pimiento
¼ cup chopped parsley
½ teaspoon dried sweet basil
3 tablespoons **HEALTH VALLEY® Safflower Oil**
1 teaspoon minced garlic
2 cups (⅔ package) grated **HEALTH VALLEY® Raw Milk Medium Cheddar Cheese**

Cook spaghetti according to directions on package. While spaghetti is cooking, combine in a bowl the walnuts, olives, pimiento, parsley and basil.

When spaghetti is done, drain immediately into a large colander. In the empty kettle, heat oil and add garlic. Sauté briefly without permitting to brown. Add spaghetti and toss to mix thoroughly. Turn into a hot serving platter, top with nut-herb mixture, sprinkle cheese over all, and serve immediately.

If desired, it can also be served with diced, browned **HEALTH VALLEY® Italian Sausages**, crumbled, cooked **HEALTH VALLEY® Bacon** or a handful of **HEALTH VALLEY® Shrimp** (thawed and drained). Total Preparation Time: 30 minutes.

Yield 4 to 6 servings

Ham Luigi

7 oz. pkg. **CREAMETTE® Spaghetti**
2 cups cooked ham, diced
6 Tbsp. butter or margarine
1 can (4 oz.) sliced mushrooms
4 Tbsp. flour
1 tsp. salt
1 can (13 oz.) evaporated milk
1 can (13¾ oz.) chicken broth
½ cup Romano or Parmesan cheese, grated
1 sweet red pepper, optional
1 green pepper, optional
1 Tbsp. butter or margarine, optional

Prepare **CREAMETTE® Spaghetti** according to package instructions. Drain. Sauté ham in butter until lightly browned. Remove ham. Add flour and salt to drippings; cook, stirring constantly for 2 minutes. Do not brown. Stir in milk, chicken broth and mushroom liquid, cook until smooth and thickened. Combine spaghetti, ham, mushrooms and sauce in 11x7x1¼ inch baking dish. Top with cheese. Bake at 350° for 20–25 minutes. (If desired, slice red and green peppers into rings; sauté in butter until soft. Garnish Ham Luigi with rings before serving.)

8 servings

Ideal Egg Spaghetti with Chicken Cacciatore

1 medium stewing chicken
¼ cup vegetable oil
1 green pepper, chopped
½ lb. mushrooms
2 onions, chopped
1 clove garlic, chopped (optional)
Salt and pepper to taste
1-8 oz. tomato sauce
1 can (No. 303) tomatoes, chopped
¼ cup Sherry wine
1 pkg. (12-oz.) **IDEAL Egg Spaghetti**

Cut chicken into segments and brown in vegetable oil using large skillet. Remove chicken and use pan to sauté green pepper, mushrooms, onions and garlic. In a large saucepan pour tomatoes and all other ingredients except chicken, **IDEAL Egg Spaghetti** and Sherry wine. Bring to a boil. Add chicken and Sherry wine. Allow to simmer with cover about 30 minutes. Cook **IDEAL Egg Spaghetti** according to package directions, and drain. Serve with sauce arranging chicken in the middle of plate. *Serves 4-6*

PERDUE

Boneless Breasts Primevera

2 whole **PERDUE® Boneless Chicken Breasts,**
  halved
3 tablespoons olive oil
1 package (4 ounces) sliced ham, cut in strips
1½ cups sliced zucchini
1 medium onion, chopped
1 package (8 ounces) thin spaghetti, cooked and
  drained
¾ cup half and half
¼ cup grated Parmesan cheese
¼ cup chopped pimiento

Wash chicken; pat dry. Cut into cubes. In Dutch oven, brown chicken in oil. Add ham, zucchini and onion. Cook until zucchini is just tender. Add remaining ingredients. Toss to blend. Simmer 5 minutes. *Serves 6*

Spaghetti with Meat Sauce

1½ pounds **FOULDS' Spaghetti**
2½ tablespoons salt
6-9 quarts boiling water
½ pound sweet Italian sausage, cut up
2 medium onions, quartered
2 cloves garlic
1 small rib celery, halved
1 small carrot, quartered
3 sprigs parsley
1½ pounds ground beef
1 can (28 ounces) tomatoes
2 jars (15½ ounces each) marinara sauce

Gradually add spaghetti and salt to rapidly boiling water so that water continues to boil. Cook uncovered, stirring occasionally, until tender. Drain in colander. While spaghetti is cooking, pro-

cess, until finely chopped, sausage, onions, garlic, celery, carrot and parsley with cutting blade in food processor. Brown sausage mixture and ground meat in Dutch oven or large pot. Add tomatoes and marinara sauce. Heat to boiling. Serve with spaghetti. *Makes 12 servings*

CONVENTIONAL METHOD:
Finely chop sausage, onions, garlic, celery, carrot and parsley. Proceed as above.

Secret Spaghetti Sauce

1¼ lb. ground beef
1 lb. Italian sausage
1 large onion, chopped
2 cloves garlic, minced (1½ teaspoons)
2 cans (1 lb. 12 oz.) whole tomatoes
2 cans (6 oz.) tomato paste
1 can (15 oz.) tomato sauce
1 cup bouillon (or red table wine)
2½ teaspoons salt
½ teaspoon pepper
2 teaspoons sugar
1 teaspoon basil
1½ teaspoons oregano leaves
2 small bay leaves, crumbled
1 tablespoon **ANGOSTURA® Aromatic Bitters**
½ lb. fresh mushrooms, sliced
¾ cup grated Parmesan cheese

Brown ground beef and Italian sausage in large heavy skillet until meat is browned, about 5 to 8 minutes. Add onion, and garlic; cook until onions are limp, about 5 minutes. Stir in tomatoes, tomato paste, tomato sauce, bouillon or wine, salt, pepper, sugar, basil, oregano leaves, bay leaves and **ANGOSTURA® Bitters**. Simmer, uncovered, over low heat until sauce thickens, about 2½ hours. Adjust seasonings to taste. Stir occasionally to prevent sticking. Add mushrooms and Parmesan cheese. Continue cooking, stirring frequently, 30 minutes longer.

Cook spaghetti as directed on package; rinse and drain. Toss with 2 tablespoons butter and 3 tablespoons Parmesan cheese. Spoon meat sauce over spaghetti; sprinkle lightly with additional Parmesan cheese and garnish with parsley. *Yield: 8 to 10 servings*

Cotto Salami Spaghetti

2 packages (8 oz. each) **OSCAR MAYER Cotto
  Salami**
1 can (4 oz.) mushrooms, drained
½ cup chopped onion
¼ cup chopped green pepper
2 tablespoons butter
2 cans (8 oz. each) tomato sauce
1 can (6 oz.) tomato paste
½ cup water
1½ teaspoons Worcestershire sauce
⅛ teaspoon pepper
8 oz. spaghetti, cooked

Cut slices of meat into wedges. In a skillet, cook mushrooms, onion and green pepper in butter until tender. Stir in meat pieces, tomato sauce, tomato paste, water, Worcestershire sauce & pepper. Cover and cook slowly 30 minutes. Serve over spaghetti. *Makes six servings*

JIMMY DEAN

Easy Sausage Spaghetti

1 lb. **JIMMY DEAN® Sausage**
2 cans condensed cream of mushroom soup
1 cup milk
4 or 5 cups zucchini (about 1½ lb.)
¼ lb. mushrooms, sliced
¼ cup sliced green onions
½ tsp. salt
¼ tsp. pepper
1 lb. spaghetti
Parmesan cheese

Brown sausage in large skillet. Break up with fork. Add zucchini, mushrooms, green onions and sauté a few more minutes. Stir in soup and milk. Season with salt and pepper to taste. Cook over medium heat 15 minutes or until zucchini is tender. (Add more milk if the mixture becomes too thick.)

Cook spaghetti and drain. Toss sausage mixture with cooked spaghetti and sprinkle generously with Parmesan cheese.

Garden Spaghetti

1 (10 oz.) package frozen chopped broccoli, thawed
  and well drained
½ pound carrots or zucchini, sliced, cooked and
  drained
1 (4 oz.) can mushroom stems and pieces, drained
¼ cup chopped onion
1 clove garlic, finely chopped
3 tablespoons low calorie margarine
3 tablespoons flour
1 teaspoon salt
½ teaspoon thyme or oregano leaves
2 cups skim milk
6 slices low calorie cheese cut into small pieces
1 (7 oz.) package **CREAMETTE® Italian Style
  Spaghetti,** cooked as package directs and drained

In large saucepan, cook onion and garlic in margarine until tender. Stir in flour, salt and thyme. Gradually stir in milk. Cook and stir over medium heat until mixture thickens. Stir in cheese product. Cook and stir until melted. Add broccoli, carrots and mushrooms; heat through. Serve over hot cooked spaghetti. Refrigerate leftovers.
Makes 6 servings

Beans and Spaghetti Carbonara

3 ounces vermicelli or thin spaghetti
½ cup diced cooked ham
1 tablespoon butter or margarine
1 package (10 oz.) **BIRDS EYE® Italian Style
  Vegetables with a Seasoned Sauce**
½ cup water
2 eggs, slightly beaten
3 tablespoons milk
3 tablespoons grated Parmesan cheese

Cook vermicelli as directed on package; drain. Sauté ham in butter in skillet. Add vegetables and water. Bring to a *full* boil over medium heat, separating vegetables with a fork and stirring occasionally. Reduce heat, cover and simmer 3 minutes. Remove from heat and stir in vermicelli. Combine eggs and milk and stir into vegetable mixture. Heat gently over low heat just until slightly thickened, about 2 minutes. Sprinkle with cheese.
Makes 3½ cups or 3 servings

MICROWAVE METHOD:
Omit water. Place ham, butter and vegetables in 1½-quart non-metal casserole. Cover, place in microwave oven and cook at high power for 3 to 4 minutes. Stir; then mix in cooked vermicelli, eggs and milk. Cover and cook for 2 to 3 minutes, or until slightly thickened, mixing lightly every minute. Sprinkle with cheese.

Pasta Primavera

⅓ cup **MAZOLA® Corn Oil**
¼ pound mushrooms, sliced (1½ cups)
1 medium onion, cut into very thin wedges (about ½
  cup)
2 cloves garlic, minced or pressed
½ pound broccoli, cut into flowerets (2 cups)
1 medium zucchini, sliced, halved (2 cups)
2 carrots, cut into julienne strips (1 cup)
⅓ cup dry white wine
¼ cup chopped parsley
1 teaspoon dried basil leaves
½ teaspoon salt
⅛ teaspoon pepper
½ pound spaghetti, cooked
½ cup grated Parmesan cheese

In large skillet heat corn oil over medium-high heat. Add mushrooms, onion and garlic; stirring frequently, cook 1 to 2 minutes. Add broccoli, zucchini and carrots; stirring frequently, cook 2 to 3 minutes. Stir in wine, parsley, basil, salt and pepper. Simmer 4 to 5 minutes or until vegetables are tender-crisp. Toss together hot cooked spaghetti, vegetable sauce and cheese.
Makes 4 to 6 servings

Vegetarian Spaghetti

2 tablespoons corn oil margarine
1 tablespoon olive oil
3 garlic cloves, finely chopped
1 cup grated raw carrots (2 carrots)
1 cup finely chopped onion (1 large onion)
1 cup sliced fresh mushrooms (¼ pound)
¼ cup finely chopped parsley
1 28-ounce can Italian tomatoes plus all the juice from
  the can
1 8-ounce can tomato sauce
1 teaspoon oregano
¼ teaspoon tarragon
¼ teaspoon sweet basil
½ teaspoon **SWEETLITE™ Fructose**
½ teaspoon salt
¼ teaspoon freshly ground black pepper
¾ cup grated Romano or Parmesan cheese
4½ cups cooked spaghetti (½ pound dry spaghetti)

Heat the margarine and olive oil in a large skillet. Add the garlic and carrots and cook over medium heat stirring occasionally for 10 minutes. Add the onion, mushrooms and parsley and continue cooking for another 10 minutes. Add all other ingredients except the grated cheese and the spaghetti and cook, covered, for 30 minutes longer. Add the grated cheese and mix well. Spoon the spaghetti sauce over the cooked spaghetti. The sauce can be prepared the day before and reheated just before serving.

Makes 6 servings

Each serving contains approximately:
½ medium fat meat exchange
1½ bread exchanges
1½ fat exchanges
1½ vegetable exchanges
267 calories
7 mg. cholesterol

Red Cross® Spaghetti with Parsley-Cheese Pesto Sauce

4 ounces **RED CROSS® Spaghetti**
1½ tsp. salt
1½ quarts boiling water
¼ cup olive oil
½ cup parsley sprigs
¼ cup grated Parmesan cheese
1 Tbsp. water
¾ tsp. dried basil
1 clove garlic

Gradually add **RED CROSS® Spaghetti** and salt to rapidly boiling water so that water continues to boil. Cook uncovered, stirring occasionally, until tender. Drain in colander. Meanwhile, combine olive oil, parsley, cheese, water, basil and garlic in electric blender or food processor. Blend at medium speed until smooth, stirring down sides of container as necessary. Return Spaghetti to cooking pot, add parsley sauce. Cook and stir until heated. Serve immediately.

Serves 2

Spaghetti Al Pesto

8 ounces (½ package) **LA ROSA® Spaghetti**
1 clove garlic, minced
⅓ cup olive oil
1 cup firmly packed fresh basil leaves OR parsley sprigs
½ cup grated Parmesan cheese
2 tablespoons pine nuts OR coarsely chopped walnuts
1 tablespoon butter
½ teaspoon salt
⅛ teaspoon pepper
Additional grated Parmesan cheese

Cook garlic in olive oil until lightly browned. Combine with remaining ingredients in electric blender; blend at high speed to a pastelike consistency, about 1 minute. Cook Spaghetti as directed on package; drain. Serve sauce over cooked Spaghetti with additional Parmesan cheese.

Serves 4

Note: To prepare Al Pesto by hand, crush basil or parsley with a mortar and pestle until pastelike. Work in salt and pepper, garlic, nuts and butter. Add olive oil a little at a time. Mix in the ½ cup grated Parmesan cheese.

Fettuccine

IMPORTED
SWISS CHEESE

Special Fettucine 'n Cheese

¼ pound prosciutto, cut into thin strips
½ pound mushrooms, sliced
¾ cup (1½ sticks) butter or margarine
1 pound fettucine
2 chicken bouillon cubes
1 cup shredded **FINLANDIA Swiss Cheese**
2 tablespoons Parmesan cheese
3 tablespoons heavy cream

Sauté ham and mushrooms in 2 tablespoons butter until mushrooms are lightly browned. Meanwhile, cook noodles in boiling water with chicken bouillon cubes for 8 minutes; drain. Add fettucine to mushrooms. Add remaining butter, cheeses and cream. Heat, stirring for 2 to 3 minutes. *Makes 4 to 6 servings*

San Giorgio®

Fettuccini with Pesto Sauce

4 cups raw fresh spinach
1 cup fresh parsley
¾ cup grated Parmesan cheese
½ cup walnuts
½ cup olive oil
1 clove garlic
½ teaspoon salt
¼ teaspoon pepper
1 box (12 ounces) **SAN GIORGIO® Fettuccini,** uncooked
Parmesan cheese (optional)

Combine spinach, parsley, Parmesan cheese, walnuts, olive oil, garlic, salt and pepper in food processor or blender container. Process or blend until mixture is smooth. Cook Fettuccini according to package directions; drain well. Immediately toss hot Fettuccini with pesto sauce in large serving dish until Fettuccini is well coated. Garnish with additional Parmesan cheese. Serve.

4 to 6 servings

Fettuccine Alfredo

1 package **RONZONI® Extra Long Fettuccine**
½ cup grated Parmesan cheese
⅔ cup light cream (sour cream may be substituted)
¼ lb. butter (preferably sweet)
1 egg yolk

Cook noodles according to directions on the panel. While noodles are cooking, beat egg yolk lightly with fork and add to cream. Melt butter. Place drained, hot noodles in warm serving bowl or platter. Pour over the noodles egg and cream mixture, melted butter and about half of the grated cheese. Toss noodles with fork and spoon until well blended, adding balance of cheese a little at a time while tossing. Top with additional grated cheese, if desired, and serve immediately.

Pasta with Carbonara Sauce

4 eggs
¼ cup butter or margarine
¼ cup cream
1 lb. fettucini or spaghetti
2 3½ oz. pkgs. **HORMEL Sliced Pepperoni**
1 cup Parmesan cheese, grated
¼ cup snipped fresh parsley
Pepper to taste

Let eggs, butter or margarine and cream stand at room temperature for 2-3 hours. Beat together eggs and cream just until blended. Add pasta to a large amount of boiling, salted water. Cook 10-12 minutes or until tender, but firm. Drain well.

Heat an ovenproof serving dish in a 250°F. oven. Turn pasta into heated serving dish. Toss pasta with butter and pepperoni. Pour egg mixture over and toss until pasta is well coated. Add cheese and parsley; toss to mix. Serve immediately.

Makes 10-12 side dishes or 4-5 main servings

Creamy Tuna Fettucini

1 can (9¼ oz.) **BUMBLE BEE® Chunk Light Tuna***
8 ounces spinach noodles
Boiling water
4 tablespoons butter
2 tablespoons olive oil
2 cloves garlic, pressed
1½ cups sliced **DOLE® Fresh Mushrooms**
1 to 1½ cups dairy sour cream
½ cup grated Romano cheese
1 tablespoon chopped parsley

Drain tuna. Cook noodles in boiling water according to package directions until just tender. Drain. Heat butter and oil in saucepan and sauté garlic and mushrooms. Blend in sour cream and cheese. Fold in tuna and heat through. Serve noodles on hot platter and top with sauce. Sprinkle parsley over sauce. Toss before serving.
Makes 4 to 6 servings

*Or use 2 cans (6½ oz. each) **BUMBLE BEE® Chunk Light Tuna.**

San Giorgio®

Tomato and Basil Fettuccini

¼ cup chopped onion
1 clove garlic, minced
¼ cup olive oil
3½ cups (28-ounce can) peeled tomatoes (with liquid)
6 fresh basil leaves, chopped or 1 tablespoon dry basil
1 teaspoon salt
½ teaspoon pepper
1 box (12 ounces) **SAN GIORGIO® Fettuccini,**
  uncooked
Parmesan cheese (optional)

Sauté onion and garlic in oil in medium skillet until onion is tender, but not brown. Chop tomatoes into small pieces; reserve liquid. Add tomatoes, tomato liquid, basil, salt and pepper; bring to boil over medium heat. Reduce heat; simmer, uncovered, 15 to 20 minutes, stirring occasionally. Cook Fettuccini according to package directions; drain well. Immediately toss hot Fettuccini with tomato basil sauce in large serving dish. Garnish with Parmesan cheese, if desired. Serve.
4 to 6 servings

Butter Buds®

Spinach Noodle Fettucine

1 cup low-fat cottage cheese
½ cup plain low-fat yogurt
½ cup thinly sliced water chestnuts
½ cup toasted slivered almonds, divided
¼ cup finely chopped pimiento
1 packet **BUTTER BUDS®**
1 tablespoon chopped fresh parsley
1 tablespoon grated Parmesan cheese
¼ teaspoon oregano
¼ teaspoon basil
¼ teaspoon thyme
Freshly ground pepper to taste
8 ounces (4 cups) uncooked spinach noodles

In medium-size bowl, blend cottage cheese into yogurt. Add remaining ingredients except noodles, using only ⅓ cup almonds. Mix well. Prepare noodles according to package directions, omitting salt. Drain. In a warm pan, toss hot noodles with cheese mixture. Turn onto warm serving platter and sprinkle with remaining almonds.
4 servings

PER SERVING (1¼ cups): Calories: 300   Protein: 14gm
Carbohydrate: 40gm   Fat: 9gm   Sodium: 295mg

Pizza

Martha White Pizza

¾ cup plus 1 tablespoon lukewarm water
1 cake or package yeast
2 cups sifted **MARTHA WHITE Plain Flour**
1 teaspoon salt
2 tablespoons shortening
Pizza Sauce*
Mozzarella cheese
Toppings of your choice

Dissolve yeast in water. Combine flour and salt; then cut in shortening, as for biscuits. Stir in water and yeast mixture. Turn dough out onto lightly floured board or pastry cloth and knead just until smooth. Place in a greased bowl and grease top. Cover and let rise in a warm place until light, about 1 hour. When light, punch down and divide into 2 pieces for 12-inch pizzas or 4 pieces for 10-inch pizzas. Roll out about ¼-inch thick. Place rounds of dough on greased baking sheet or pizza pans. Crimp edges. Top with Pizza Sauce and mozzarella cheese. Add your favorite toppings. Bake at 400 degrees for about 20 minutes. Makes 2 large or 4 small pizzas.
(Continued)

For very crisp crust: Bake pizza 10 minutes on pan, then slide pizza off pan directly onto oven rack and finish baking.

Note: If using **MARTHA WHITE Self-Rising Flour**, omit salt.

*Pizza Sauce

1 6-ounce can tomato paste
1 8-ounce can tomato sauce
½ teaspoon salt
1 teaspoon Worcestershire sauce
1 teaspoon garlic salt
2 or 3 drops **TABASCO® Sauce**
½ teaspoon crushed thyme
1 teaspoon crushed oregano

Combine and mix well.

Deep Dish Pizza

Crust:
52 **RITZ Crackers**, finely rolled (about 2 cups crumbs)
¼ cup grated Parmesan cheese
¼ cup butter or margarine, softened
1 egg, slightly beaten
2 tablespoons cold water

Filling:
1 tablespoon butter or margarine
¼ cup coarsely chopped onion
¼ cup coarsely chopped green pepper
1 clove garlic, minced
1 (16-ounce) can whole peeled tomatoes, undrained, cut up
1 (6-ounce) can tomato paste
1 (4-ounce) can sliced mushrooms, drained
½ teaspoon basil
½ teaspoon marjoram
½ teaspoon oregano
4 ounces mozzarella cheese, grated (about 1 cup)
1 tablespoon grated Parmesan cheese

1. **Make Crust:** Preheat oven to 325° F.
2. In medium bowl, using fork or pastry blender, combine **RITZ Cracker** crumbs, Parmesan cheese and butter or margarine; mix in egg and water until thoroughly blended. Using back of large spoon, press onto bottom and sides of 9-inch pie plate to form crust. Bake 10 minutes.
3. **Make Filling:** In medium saucepan, over medium heat, melt butter or margarine; sauté onion, green pepper and garlic about 5 minutes, or until tender.
4. Add tomatoes, tomato paste, mushrooms, basil, marjoram and oregano; heat thoroughly. Spoon into crust; top with mozzarella cheese and Parmesan cheese. Bake 20 to 25 minutes, or until bubbly.
5. **To Serve:** Let stand 5 minutes; cut into wedges.

Makes 4 to 6 servings

MICROWAVE METHOD:
1. Prepare crust as in Step 2. Press into 9-inch microwave-proof pie plate. Microwave at 100% power 5 to 6 minutes, rotating ½ turn after 3 minutes, until crust is no longer moist.
2. In 3-quart microwave-proof bowl, microwave butter or margarine, onion, green pepper and garlic at 100% power 4 to 5

minutes, stirring after 3 minutes, until vegetables are tender. Stir in tomatoes, tomato paste, mushrooms, basil, marjoram and oregano; microwave at 100% power 5 minutes, stirring after 3 minutes.
3. Assemble pie as in Step 4; microwave at 100% power 3 minutes. Serve as in Step 5.

Merry Pizza Rounds

1 can of your favorite pizza or spaghetti sauce
1 pound **BORDEN® Mozzarella Cheese**
1 pound **OSCAR MAYER Jumbo Franks**
5 **BAYS® English Muffins**, split

Cut 10 deep crosswise slits along one side of each frankfurter without cutting completely through. Broil 2 to 3 minutes or until lightly browned. Cut 10 round thin slices of cheese about 1 ounce each and place on muffins. Broil 2 minutes, or until melted. Place one hot dog on each muffin and top with 2 tablespoons sauce. Fill center with remaining grated cheese, sprinkle with a pinch of oregano. Broil 2 minutes more. *Makes 10 servings*

Favorite recipe from **National Hot Dog & Sausage Council**

King Arthur Pizza

1 cup lukewarm water
1 teaspoon sugar
1 teaspoon salt
2 tablespoons salad oil
1 package dry yeast
3 to 3½ cups **KING ARTHUR Flour**

Place first 5 ingredients in a bowl, add 1 cup of flour and beat for 2 minutes with electric beater. Gradually add balance of flour, stirring by hand, until the dough no longer sticks to the sides of the bowl.

Place dough on lightly floured board and knead for 5 minutes. Place in greased bowl, turning over to grease top, cover and let rise in a warm place until double in bulk.

Mix together:
1 can (6-oz.) or ⅔ cup tomato paste
½ cup water
1 teaspoon salt
1 teaspoon crushed oregano
Dash pepper

When dough has doubled in bulk, punch down, divide in half. Form each half into a ball, handling as little as possible. Grease a 12 inch pizza pan, set 1 ball of dough on it and then let it rest for 2 or 3 minutes, to relax the gluten. Then press out the dough with your knuckles and with the back of your fingers to cover the pan. Make the edges raised and slightly thick.

On each circle of dough:

Arrange:
¼ pound mozzarella cheese sliced about ⅛ inch thick
Spread evenly:
½ tomato mixture
Sprinkle evenly:
2 tablespoons olive or salad oil
2 tablespoons grated Parmesan cheese

Bake 25 minutes in a 400 degree oven. Serve hot.

Pizza

1 package active dry yeast
¼ cup warm water (110°F)
½ cup milk, scalded
¼ cup vegetable oil
1 teaspoon salt
¾ cup **3-MINUTE BRAND®** Oats or 2 packets
  Regular Flavor HARVEST® Instant Oatmeal
1½ to 2 cups all-purpose flour
1 8-ounce can tomato sauce
2 tablespoons dry parsley flakes
2 tablespoons instant minced dry onion
1 teaspoon oregano leaves
⅛ teaspoon garlic salt
1 pound ground beef or sausage, browned
Other toppings as desired, such as mushrooms, green
  peppers
2 cups (8 ounces) shredded mozzarella cheese
¼ cup grated Parmesan or Romano cheese

Sprinkle yeast over warm water; set aside. Add oil and salt to scalded milk; let cool to lukewarm. Stir in yeast, oats, and 1¼ cups of the flour. On lightly floured surface, knead in enough of the remaining flour to form a stiff dough. Press dough onto 2 greased pizza pans, or form 8 6-inch rounds on greased baking sheets. Combine tomato sauce, parsley, onion, oregano, and garlic salt. Spread on crusts. Sprinkle beef and/or other toppings over sauce, then top with the cheeses. Bake in a 425°F. oven for 15 to 20 minutes or till crust is brown and crisp.

VARIATION:

Pizza Pinwheels

Prepare crust and sauce as above. Pat dough out to 2 15 x 9-inch rectangles. Spread with sauce; sprinkle beef atop. Beginning at a long end, roll up jelly-roll style. Slice into 1-inch slices. Place, cut side down, on greased baking sheet. Bake in a 350°F. oven about 25 minutes. Sprinkle cheese atop slices. Return to oven till cheese is melted. *Makes about 2 dozen Pizza Pinwheels*

Sausage Pizza

6 oz. can tomato paste
½ tsp. garlic salt
½ tsp. oregano
¼ tsp. basil
3 cups shredded Cheddar or mozzarella cheese or both
1 lb. **BOB EVANS FARMS® Roll Sausage**
1 small can mushroom stems and pieces, drained
6 to 8 stuffed green olives, sliced
8 English muffins or 1 loaf Italian bread

Partially brown sausage and drain. Thin tomato paste with a little water and mix with seasonings. Spread on muffins or bread cut lengthwise. Add most of cheese, then sausage, mushrooms and olives. Sprinkle remaining cheese. Bake in preheated 425° oven about 15 to 20 minutes. *(Continued)*

VARIATION:

1 lb. **BOB EVANS FARMS® Roll Sausage** or **Italian**-partially brown and drain. Sprinkle on top of your favorite brand frozen pizza.

Rhodes™ Chicago-Style Deep Dish Pizza

1 loaf **RHODES™ White** or **Honey Wheat Dough,**
  thawed
Olive oil or vegetable oil
Cornmeal
1 lb. bulk pork sausage, cooked and drained
1 can (1 lb. 20 oz.) peeled whole tomatoes, drained
1 teaspoon basil
1 teaspoon oregano
12 ounces mozzarella cheese, thinly sliced
1 green pepper, thinly sliced, optional
1 cup sliced ripe olives, optional
½ cup grated Parmesan cheese

Let dough rise in warm place 30 to 40 minutes. Grease 12-inch deep-dish pizza pan, 9x12-inch cake pan, or 12-inch oven-proof skillet. Sprinkle lightly with cornmeal. Pat out dough to fit bottom and up sides of pan. Prick with a fork and bake in a 425°F. oven for 7 minutes. Lightly mash tomatoes and mix with oregano and basil. Drizzle small amount of olive oil over partially baked crust. Arrange sliced mozzarella over crust. Add in layers; crumbled pork sausage, tomato mixture, green peppers and olives. Sprinkle Parmesan cheese over all. Bake at 425°F. 45 minutes. Let stand 5 minutes before serving.

Hunt's
Shortcut Pizzas

2 (1-lb.) loaves frozen enriched bread dough
1 (15-oz.) can **HUNT'S®** Tomato Sauce
¼ cup grated Parmesan cheese
2 tsp. Italian herb seasoning
1 tsp. seasoned salt
½ tsp. garlic powder
½ tsp. sugar
3 cups shredded mozzarella cheese

Suggested Toppings:
Crumbled Italian sausage
Thinly sliced Italian dry salami and pepperoni
Strips of bell pepper
Thinly sliced onion rings
Sliced mushrooms
Sliced ripe olives
Diced canned green chilies
Anchovies

Thaw loaves of bread dough according to package directions. Roll out each loaf on a lightly floured surface to fit a 15-inch pizza or jelly roll pan. Combine **HUNT'S® Tomato Sauce**, Parmesan cheese, Italian seasoning, salt, garlic powder and sugar; mix well. Use *half* the sauce mixture to coat the entire surface of each pizza. Sprinkle each with *1½ cups* cheese. Top with any or all of suggested toppings. Bake at 450° 12 to 15 minutes.

Makes two 15-inch pizzas

Fettuccini with Pesto Sauce *(top)*, Tomato and Basil Fettuccini *(bottom)*
San Giorgio® *(San Giorgio-Skinner, Inc.)*

Bertolli® Stuffed Artichokes
Bertolli® *(Bertolli U.S.A.)*

A Little Bit of Italy
Knox®, Wish-Bone® *(Thomas J. Lipton, Inc.)*

Pizza Roll™ Pasta Snack Dip Tray
Jeno's® *(Jeno's)*

Italian Salad
Brownberry® *(Brownberry)*

Vegetable Pepperoni Salad
Stokely's®, Stokely's Finest®
(Stokely-Van Camp, Inc.)

Linguine Tuna Salad
ReaLemon® *(Borden Inc.)*

Caesar Salad
(Leafy Greens Council)

Antipasto Salad
Campbell's *(Campbell Soup Co.)*

Insalata con Tonno
Chicken of the Sea® *(Ralston Purina Co.)*

Fisherman's Favorite Cioppino Salad
Wish-Bone® *(Thomas J. Lipton, Inc.)*

Mediterranean Meatball Salad
Mazola® *(Best Foods)*

Lima Garlic Salad *(bottom)*, Insalada Pepperidge *(top)*
Pepperidge Farm® *(Pepperidge Farm, Inc.)*

Quick Italian Soup
Betty Crocker® **Hamburger Helper**® *(General Mills, Inc.)*

Italian Minestrone Soup
Coca-Cola® *(The Coca-Cola Company)*

Roaster Marinara
Perdue® *(Perdue Farms Inc.)*

Neapolitan Lasagne
La Rosa® *(V. La Rosa & Sons, Inc.)*

Easy Sausage Spaghetti
Jimmy Dean® *(Jimmy Dean Meat Company, Inc.)*

Ravioli Pepperonata
Chef Boy-Ar-Dee® *(American Home Foods)*

Parmesan Crumb Fillet
Booth *(Booth Fisheries Corp.)*

Deep Dish Pizza
Ritz *(Nabisco Brands, Inc.)*

Fettuccine Alfredo
Ronzoni® *(Ronzoni Macaroni Co., Inc.)*

Cornish Italiano
Tyson® *(Tyson Foods, Inc.)*

Pasta al Pesto
Armanino Farms *(Armanino Farms of California)*

39

Antipasto Sandwich
Oscar Mayer *(Oscar Mayer Foods Corporation)*

Italian Sausage Loaf
Bridgford *(Bridgford Foods Corp.)*

Rotini Tetrazzini
San Giorgio® *(San Giorgio-Skinner,Inc.)*

Veal Paprika
Delft Blue®-Provimi® *(Delft Blue-Provimi Inc*

Lasagne Roll-Ups
American Beauty®
(The Pillsbury Company)

Meatloaf Italienne
A.1. *(Heublein Inc.)*

Chicken Italienne
Wesson®, Hunt's® *(Hunt-Wesson Kitchens)*

Buttery Pasta with Shrimp
Land O Lakes® *(Land O'Lakes, Inc.)*

Pizza Style Tater Tots®
Ore-Ida® Tater Tots® *(Ore-Ida Foods, Inc.)*

Open-Face Pizza Sandwiches
Bisquick® *(General Mills, Inc.)*

Secret Spaghetti Sauce
Angostura® *(Angostura International Ltd.)*

Turkey Italiano with Vegetables
Louis Rich™ *(Louis Rich Co., Div. of Oscar Mayer Foods Corp.)*

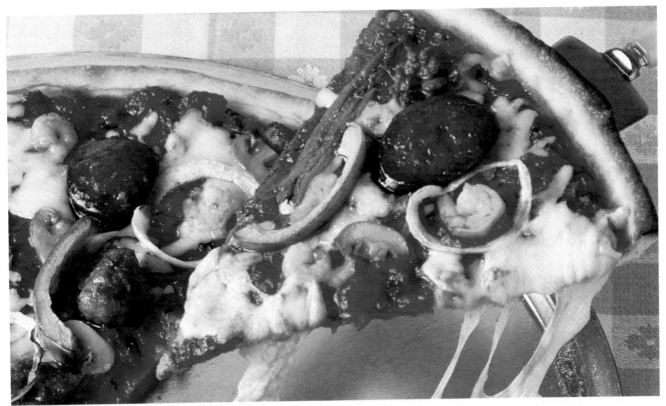

Shortcut Pizzas
Hunt's® *(Hunt-Wesson Kitchens)*

Beans and Spaghetti Carbonara
Birds Eye® *(General Foods)*

Impossible Lasagne Pie
Bisquick® *(General Mills, Inc.)*

Tuscany Sausage Skillet
Birds Eye® *(General Foods)*

Shrimp Scampi with Zucchini
Land O Lakes® *(Land O'Lakes, Inc.)*

Macaroni & Beans Italiano
Heinz *(Heinz U.S.A.)*

Steaks Italiano
Ragu´® *(Chesebrough-Pond's Inc.)*

Mueller's® Chicken Tetrazzini
Mueller's® *(C. F. Mueller Company)*

South African Rock Lobster Tetrazzini
South African Rock Lobster *(South African Rock Lobster Service Corp.)*

Italian Rice & Cheese Bake
Wyler's® *(Borden Inc.)*

44

Homestyle Pasta Bake
French's® *(R. T. French Co.)*

Green Beans Italian
Land O Lakes® *(Land O'Lakes, Inc.)*

Spinach Italienne
Keebler® Harvest Wheat *(Keebler Company)*

Cheesy-Roman Tomatoes
Pizza-Mate® *(Fisher Cheese Co.)*

Stuffed Green Peppers Provencale
Polly-O® *(Pollio Dairy Products Corp.)*

Slim Herb Mac and Cheese *(top)*, Luncheon Salad *(left)*, Garden Spaghetti *(right)*
Creamette®, Creamettes® *(The Creamette Co.)*

Vegetables Italiano *(right)*, Napoli Fruit Shake *(left)*, Ham and
Noodles Tonnarelli *(bottom)*
Del Monte *(Del Monte Corporation)*

Lemon Ice
Bertolli® *(Bertolli U.S.A.)*

Cannoli con Frutta
(Cling Peach Advisory Board)

46

Amaretto Strawberries *(left)*, Sparkling Amaretto &
Cognac *(right)*
Hiram Walker *(Hiram Walker & Sons, Inc.)*

Saronno Panettone
Amaretto Di Saronno® *(Foreign Vintages, Inc.)*

Pineapple Tortoni Sicilian
Dole® *(Castle & Cooke Foods)*

Tortoni Mold
Eagle®, Borden® *(Borden Inc.)*

Saronno Zuccotto
Amaretto Di Saronno® *(Foreign Vintages, Inc.)*

Blueberry Zuppa Inglese
(North American Blueberry Council)

Apricot Choco-Nilla Cheesecake
(California Apricot Advisory Board)

48

Deep Dish Pizz-A-Roni

1 pkg. (8 oz.) **GOLDEN GRAIN®** Beef Flavor
  RICE-A-RONI®
2 Tbsp. butter or margarine
2¾ cups hot water
1 cup grated Cheddar cheese
1 cup spaghetti sauce
8 slices Jack cheese
2 Italian sausage, cooked and sliced
2 Tbsp. grated Parmesan cheese
1 can (2½ oz.) sliced mushrooms, drained

Prepare **RICE-A-RONI®** with butter and water, according to package directions. Let stand until all liquid is absorbed. Fold in Cheddar cheese. Spread into 10-inch pie plate. Bake at 450°F. for five minutes to set crust. Top with spaghetti sauce, sliced cheese, sausage, Parmesan, mushrooms. Top with additional sauce, if desired. Bake at 450°F. for 10 minutes or until lightly brown. Let stand 5 minutes before cutting into 8 wedges.

Budweiser.

Beer Drinker's Deep-Pan Pizza

Crust:
1 cup warm **BUDWEISER®** Beer
4 tablespoons olive or salad oil
1 tablespoon sugar
1½ teaspoons salt
1 package active dry yeast
2¾ to 3¼ cups all-purpose flour
2 tablespoons cornmeal

Topping:
10 to 12 ounces mozzarella cheese, shredded or thinly
  sliced
1 can (6 ounces) tomato paste
½ cup **BUDWEISER®** Beer
2 teaspoons oregano
1 teaspoon fennel seed (optional)
½ teaspoon sugar
¾ to 1 pound bulk pork or Italian sausage, broken up
½ cup grated Parmesan cheese

For crust, combine in a large bowl the warm **BUDWEISER®** Beer, 2 tablespoons oil, sugar, salt, and yeast. Add 1½ cups flour; beat until smooth. Stir in enough additional flour to make a fairly stiff dough. Turn dough out onto a lightly floured surface. Knead until smooth and elastic (about 5 minutes). Place dough in a greased bowl, turning once to grease top. Cover and let rise in warm place (85°F) until double in bulk (about 1 hour). Punch dough down. (For 2 small pizzas, divide in half.) Using 2 tablespoons oil, coat a 14-inch round deep pizza pan. (Or use two 9-inch round cake pans). Sprinkle with cornmeal. Pat dough into pan, pinching up a rim around the edge. Cover and let rise in a warm place until double in bulk (about 30 minutes).

For topping, mix tomato paste, **BUDWEISER®** Beer, oregano, fennel seed, and sugar. Cover pizza dough evenly with mozzarella cheese; evenly spoon on tomato paste mixture. Sprinkle with sausage, then top with Parmesan cheese. Bake at 450°F 15 to 20 minutes, or until crust is browned and sausage is cooked.
Serves 4

Falbo's Pizza

Dough: for 2-12 in. Crusts
1 pkg. dry yeast
¼ cup lukewarm water
⅔ cup lukewarm water
¾ tsp. salt
2 Tbsp. vegetable oil
1 tsp. sugar
About 3 cups flour

Dissolve yeast in ¼ cup of water. Blend water, salt, oil, sugar and dissolved yeast. Then add flour in small amounts and work in until the dough is smooth and only slightly sticky. Place in a lightly greased bowl, turn to coat the dough. Set in a warm place and allow to raise until double the original size (about 2 hours).

Punch down, divide into two balls. Roll out to fit each 12 inch pan or two 9½x13½ in. pans. Pans should be lightly greased.

Sauce and Topping for two Pizzas:
1½ cups tomato puree
½ cup water
¾ tsp. salt
⅛ tsp. black pepper
½ tsp. sweet basil
⅛ tsp. garlic salt
2 Tbsp. **FALBO'S** Romano or **Parmesan Cheese**
1 lb. **FALBO'S** Mozzarella or **Scamorza**, shredded
1 tsp. oregano

Combine puree, water, salt, pepper, basil, garlic and grated cheese. Spread ½ of the mixture on each pizza crust, cover with mozzarella and sprinkle with oregano. Bake in a preheated 500 degree oven on the bottom shelf for 10-20 min. or until the crust is crisp and the cheese is melted.

Note: Sausage should be put on raw and before the cheese. All other desired ingredients such as anchovies, mushrooms, etc. should also be put on before the cheese.

Easy Pizza Napoli

3 cups biscuit mix
1½ cups beer or water
1 jar (15 ounces) pizza sauce
2 cups (about 8 ounces) shredded Cheddar cheese,
  divided
1 can (12 ounces) **SPAM®**, diced
1 can (4 ounces) mushroom pieces, drained
1 small onion, thinly sliced
1 large green pepper, seeded and cut in 12 rings
1 teaspoon oregano

In medium bowl, stir together biscuit mix and beer until well mixed. Spread batter over bottom of greased 15 x 10 x 1-inch jelly-roll pan. Drizzle sauce over batter; spread carefully to cover surface. Sprinkle with ½ the cheese. Top with **SPAM®**, mushrooms, and onion. Arrange green pepper rings over surface to mark 12 separate portions. Sprinkle with remaining cheese and oregano. Bake in 425° F oven 25 to 30 minutes, until crust is golden brown. Let stand 5 minutes before slicing. *12 servings*

Open-Face Pizza Sandwiches

2 cups **BISQUICK® Baking Mix**
½ cup cold water
1 pound ground beef
½ cup grated Parmesan cheese
¼ cup chopped onion
2 tablespoons chopped green pepper
1 teaspoon salt
1 teaspoon dried oregano leaves
⅛ teaspoon pepper
2 cans (6 ounces each) tomato paste
2 to 3 tomatoes, thinly sliced
8 slices mozzarella cheese (each about 4x4 inches), cut diagonally into halves

Heat oven to 450°. Mix baking mix and water until soft dough forms; beat vigorously 20 strokes. Divide dough into halves. Pat each half into rectangle, 16x4 inches, on greased cookie sheet with floured hands. Bake until light brown, 8 to 10 minutes.

Reduce oven temperature to 350°. Mix ground beef, Parmesan cheese, onion, green pepper, salt, oregano, pepper and tomato paste; spread over rectangles. Bake until beef is done, 20 to 25 minutes. Arrange tomatoes down center of each rectangle, overlapping edges; layer mozzarella cheese slices over tomatoes. Bake until cheese is melted, about 5 minutes longer.

About 6 servings

HIGH ALTITUDE DIRECTIONS (3500 to 6500 feet): Bake until beef is done, 25 to 30 minutes.

Fix-a-Pizza!

4 cups **FRITOS® Brand Corn Chips**
½ pound mozzarella cheese, sliced thin
1 pound ground beef
1 clove garlic, minced
1 12-ounce can tomato paste
1 teaspoon salt
¼ teaspoon black pepper
1 teaspoon oregano
1 3-ounce can mushrooms, drained and sliced
3 eggs, well beaten
½ cup canned tomatoes, drained and cut into pieces
1 2-ounce can anchovies
½ cup grated sharp Cheddar cheese
¼ cup grated Parmesan cheese

Arrange the **FRITOS® Brand Corn Chips** in a 12-inch pizza pan. Cover with mozzarella cheese slices. Sauté ground beef with garlic until light brown. Add tomato paste, salt, pepper, oregano, mushrooms and eggs. Mix well. Spread beef mixture over cheese. Sprinkle with tomato pieces, Cheddar cheese, and anchovies. Top with Parmesan cheese. Bake at 375°F. for 20 minutes.

Makes 1 12-inch pizza

Pizza Bread

1 pkg. dry yeast
¼ cup sugar
1 tsp. garlic salt
1 tsp. basil
1 tsp. oregano
3½ cups flour
½ cup **COUNTY LINE® Cheddar Cheese**, grated
½ cup **COUNTY LINE® Monterey Jack Cheese**, grated
1 cup milk
¼ cup butter
¼ cup water
1 egg

Mix dry ingredients together. Mix milk, butter, and water; heat until butter melts over top. Add one egg. Add wet ingredients to dry ingredients, and mix well. Place in covered bowl in refrigerator for 2 hours to 4 days. Roll dough into rectangle. Sprinkle with grated **COUNTY LINE® Cheddar Cheese** and **COUNTY LINE® Monterey Jack Cheese**. Roll up and put into bread pan. Cover. Let rise in warm place for 1 hour, or until double in size. Bake 20 minutes at 375°.

ᴅurꜰee

French Bread Pizza

1 package (1¼ oz.) **DURKEE Spaghetti Sauce Mix**
1¾ cups water
1 can (6 oz.) tomato paste
2 loaves French bread, split in half lengthwise
½ pound bulk Italian sausage, fried and crumbled
1 can (4 oz.) mushroom stems and pieces, drained
4 oz. thinly sliced pepperoni
1½ cups (6 oz.) shredded mozzarella cheese

Prepare sauce mix according to package directions, keep warm. Cut each split loaf in quarters and place on baking sheet cut side up; spread with sauce. Top with sausage, mushrooms, pepperoni and cheese. Bake at 375°F for 15 minutes or until heated through.

Makes 8 servings

Meat

Beef

RAGU´

Steaks Italiano

3 tablespoons vegetable oil
1 medium onion, sliced
1 medium green pepper, chopped
8 rump steaks (about 1 pound), pounded to ¼-inch thick
1 jar (15½ oz.) **RAGU´® Homestyle Spaghetti Sauce,** any flavor
Salt and pepper, to taste
1½ cups (6 oz.) shredded mozzarella cheese

In large skillet, sauté onion and green pepper in oil until onion is translucent; remove from skillet. Add steaks to skillet and brown quickly on both sides. Return onion and pepper to skillet. Add **Homestyle Spaghetti Sauce**, salt and pepper; simmer 10 minutes. Sprinkle evenly with mozzarella. Cover and simmer 8-10 minutes more. Serve on pasta. *Serves 4*

Elena's Round Steak Rolls

1½ lb. round steak—½ inch thick
6 slices bacon
1 cup Italian style bread crumbs
2 cloves garlic finely chopped
1-2 tablespoons dry or fresh parsley (chop fresh parsley finely)
⅓ cup Parmesan cheese
½ tsp. salt
⅛ tsp. black or hot pepper
2-3 tablespoons **PASTORELLI® Regina Olive Oil**
1 **PASTORELLI® Italian-Chef Spaghetti Sauce** or
   1-8 oz. **Pizza Sauce**

Cut round steak into 6 pieces; then pound with meat hammer or heavy edged utensil until nearly paper thin. Sauté bacon slices until they are not quite crisp. Place one slice of bacon on each piece of meat. Combine the bread crumbs, garlic, parsley, cheese, and seasonings, then spoon this mixture on top of bacon slice. Roll each piece, being sure mixture is sealed within the steak roll. Heat enough **Regina Olive Oil** to cover thinly the bottom of the pan. Place steak rolls in pan, cover with the choice of your favorite **Italian-Chef Sauce** . . . **Pizza** or **Spaghetti**. Cover skillet, simmer for one to one and a half hours til tender. Serve with side dish of your choice. *4-6 servings*

**Libby's
Libby's
Libby's®**

Italian Stuffed Flank Steak

2 flank steaks (1 lb. ea.)
1 egg
1 tablespoon water
5 slices white bread, cubed
1 cup shredded mozzarella cheese (about 4 oz.)
¼ cup chopped onion
2 tablespoons grated Parmesan cheese
1½ teaspoons parsley flakes
½ teaspoon salt
½ teaspoon oregano
¼ teaspoon pepper
1½ cups **LIBBY'S® Tomato Juice**
½ teaspoon oregano
3 drops hot pepper sauce

Preheat oven to 350°F. Make shallow diagonal cuts on one side of each flank steak. Combine egg and water; stir in next eight ingredients. On uncut side, spread half of mixture on center of each steak. Roll steaks up lengthwise; tie securely, closing ends with skewers. Place in roasting pan. Combine tomato juice, oregano and hot pepper sauce; pour over steaks. Cook, covered, about 2 hours; uncover and cook an additional 30 minutes or until meat is tender, basting frequently with tomato juice mixture (add additional juice if necessary). *Yields 6 to 8 servings*

Italian Beef Casserole

4 cups cooked and drained macaroni
1 2½ oz. package **BUDDIG Peppered Beef**, shredded
1 medium zucchini, sliced
1 can (1 lb., 4 oz.) white kidney beans, drained
1 can (16 oz.) stewed tomatoes
2 cans (8 oz.) tomato sauce
2 carrots, shredded
1 tablespoon Italian seasoning
1 teaspoon garlic powder
½ cup shredded mozzarella cheese

Combine all ingredients except cheese in greased 3-quart casserole. Sprinkle cheese over top. Bake in 375° oven for 30 minutes.
Serves 4 to 6

MICROWAVE METHOD:
Prepare as above. Cook on high for 10 to 12 minutes or until bubbly hot throughout and cheese is melted. *Serves 4 to 6*

Family Pot Roast

About 3 lb. chuck roast, any cut
2 tablespoons oil
1 can (16 oz.) tomatoes
1 cup **COCA-COLA®**
1 pkg. (1½ oz.) spaghetti sauce mix
1 cup finely cut onion
¾ cup finely cut celery
1½ teaspoons salt
½ teaspoon garlic salt

In a Dutch oven, brown meat in the oil, about 10 minutes on each side. Drain off fat. Break up tomatoes in their juice; add remaining ingredients, stirring until spaghetti sauce mix is dissolved. Pour over meat. Cover, simmer slowly about 2½ hours or until meat is fork-tender. Thicken gravy and serve over sliced meat.
Makes 6 to 8 servings (about 3 cups sauce)

Italian Pot Roast

1 chuck roast, about 3 pounds
2 to 3 tablespoons grated Parmesan cheese
2 tablespoons oil
2⅓ cups water
2 cans (6-oz. each) tomato paste
1 envelope (1¾-oz.) **FRENCH'S® Thick, Homemade Style Spaghetti Sauce Mix**
¼ cup Burgundy or other dry red wine, if desired
1 bag (16-oz.) unseasoned European style mixture of vegetables such as broccoli, cauliflower and red pepper
Cooked spiral or other macaroni

Coat roast with cheese. Brown in oil in large skillet or Dutch oven-type pan; pour off excess fat. Add water, tomato paste, sauce mix and Burgundy, stirring to blend. Cover and simmer 1½ to 2 hours, or until tender. Add vegetables; cook 15 minutes. Slice roast and serve with vegetables and sauce on macaroni. *8 to 10 servings*

ANTINORI

Marchesa Antinori's Stracotto

1 medium onion
1 very small sprig rosemary
1 stalk celery
3-4 leaves fresh basil
1 bunch parsley
1 carrot
1½ lb. rolled beef
Garlic
2 slices bacon (cut into bits)
Salt and pepper to taste
1 cup **VILLA ANTINORI Red Chianti Classico**
½ can tomato paste

Chop fine onion, rosemary, celery, basil, parsley, and carrot, and brown in olive oil.

Make tiny cuts in beef at regular intervals; insert a thin slice of garlic and a bit of bacon in each cut. Rub all over with salt and pepper.

Brown meat in pan with vegetables, add wine, and slowly cook until reduced by half. Add tomato paste diluted with 1 can water. Cook slowly for 2-3 hours until beef is tender and done.

Ground Beef

Elam's

Party Polenta with Meat Sauce

Polenta:
1½ cups cold water
1½ cups **ELAM'S® Stone Ground 100% Whole Yellow Corn Meal***
¾ teaspoon salt
3 cups boiling water
1½ cups shredded Cheddar cheese
1 egg, beaten

Meat Sauce:
1 cup sliced onion
1 cup thinly sliced celery
1 cup sliced carrot
2 Tbsp. cooking oil or shortening
1 lb. ground beef (chuck or round)
1 can (1 pound) tomatoes
1 can (8 ounces) tomato sauce
1½ teaspoons salt
1½ teaspoons oregano
1 teaspoon turbinado
1 bay leaf
½ cup grated Parmesan cheese

Prepare polenta. Combine and mix cold water and corn meal. Add salt to boiling water. Add corn meal mixture to boiling water and bring to a boil, stirring constantly. Cover partially; cook slowly 7 minutes, stirring often. Stir in cheese and egg. Pour into buttered 9-inch square baking pan. Cover; chill 3 to 4 hours or overnight. Prepare sauce. Cook onion, celery and carrot in oil or shortening until onion is limp. Add beef; cook until meat is grey and crumbly. Add tomatoes, tomato sauce, salt, oregano, turbinado and bay leaf; mix well. Simmer uncovered until sauce is thickened and vegetables are tender, about 40 minutes. Remove bay leaf. Remove polenta from pan. Cut into 8 equal portions. Place in buttered shallow 3-quart baking dish. Spoon sauce over polenta. Sprinkle with Parmesan cheese. Bake in moderate oven (350° F.) until polenta is hot, about 30 minutes.   *Yield: 8 servings*

*ELAM'S® Organically Grown Stone Ground 100% Whole Yellow Corn Meal may be substituted, if desired.

Impossible Lasagne Pie

½ cup small curd creamed cottage cheese
¼ cup grated Parmesan cheese
1 pound ground beef, cooked and drained
1 cup shredded mozzarella cheese (4 ounces)
1 teaspoon dried oregano leaves
½ teaspoon dried basil leaves
1 can (6 ounces) tomato paste
1 cup milk
2 eggs
⅔ cup **BISQUICK® Baking Mix**
1 teaspoon salt
¼ teaspoon pepper

Heat oven to 400°. Grease pie plate, 10x1½ inches. Layer cottage cheese and Parmesan cheese in plate. Mix cooked beef, ½ cup of the mozzarella cheese, the oregano, basil and tomato paste; spoon evenly over top. Beat milk, eggs, baking mix, salt and pepper until smooth, 15 seconds in blender on high or 1 minute with hand beater. Pour into plate. Bake until golden brown and knife inserted in center comes out clean, 30 to 35 minutes. Sprinkle with remaining cheese. Cool 5 minutes.   *6 to 8 servings*

HIGH ALTITUDE DIRECTIONS (3500 to 6500 feet): No adjustments are necessary.

NABISCO BRANDS INC

Kabobs International

1½ pounds ground beef chuck
1 cup **NABISCO 100% Bran Cereal**
⅓ cup finely chopped onion
¼ cup water
1¾ teaspoons salt
2 cloves garlic, crushed
¼ teaspoon ground black pepper

Basting Sauce:
½ cup red wine vinegar
3 tablespoons vegetable oil
¾ teaspoon oregano

Vegetables:
2 small zucchini, cut in 1-inch pieces
18 whole fresh mushrooms
1 (4-ounce) jar **DROMEDARY Pimiento Pieces**, drained

1. In medium bowl, combine beef, **NABISCO 100% Bran Cereal**, onion, water, 1½ teaspoons salt, 1 clove garlic and pepper; mix until well blended. Moisten hands with cold water and shape mixture into 24 1-inch meatballs. Set aside.
2. In small bowl, make Basting Sauce by blending vinegar, oil, oregano, ¼ teaspoon salt and 1 clove garlic.
3. Carefully thread 6 skewers, alternating meatballs, zucchini, mushrooms and pimientos; brush well with sauce. Grill or broil in oven about 7 to 10 minutes or until desired doneness, turning occasionally and basting with remaining sauce.
4. If broiling in oven, serve with pan juices.

Makes 6 servings

Cannelloni
San Joaquin

Crepe:
1 cup flour
¼ teaspoon salt
3 eggs
2 tablespoons melted butter
1¼ cups milk
¼ cup California brandy

Filling:
2 tablespoons olive oil
¼ cup onions, chopped
1 teaspoon garlic, finely chopped
1 10-oz. package frozen chopped spinach, defrosted
  and drained
1 pound ground beef
1 teaspoon dried oregano
Salt
Pepper

White Sauce: (Besciamella)
4 tablespoons butter
4 tablespoons flour
2 cups milk
1 teaspoon salt
¼ teaspoon white pepper

Tomato Sauce:
2 tablespoons olive oil
1 small yellow onion, chopped
1 20-oz. can whole tomatoes
4 tablespoons tomato paste
½ cup California Brandy
1 tablespoon basil
1 teaspoon sugar
Salt
Pepper

Crepes: Combine flour and salt together, and add eggs mixing until there are no lumps. Add melted butter. Slowly stir in milk and brandy and mix until batter is the consistency of thin cream. Let batter settle about one hour before using. Cook the crepes in a well-buttered six-inch skillet over medium-high heat. Ladle batter into pan to cover flat surface and pour remainder back into the bowl for thin crepes. When edges begin to brown, turn and brown on other side.

Filling: Heat oil in a skillet and add onions and garlic, cooking over medium heat until they are tender. Stir in spinach and cook another five minutes. Push onion-spinach mixture to side of skillet and add ground beef, and cook until lightly browned. Add oregano, salt and pepper to taste.

White Sauce: In a saucepan melt butter, add flour and blend to a creamy consistency. Pour in milk and cook until mixture bubbles and thickens. Add salt and pepper.

Tomato Sauce: Heat oil in a saucepan and sauté onion until tender. Chop tomatoes and add with tomato paste to pan. Heat and add brandy, basil, sugar. Salt and pepper to taste.

TO ASSEMBLE:
Preheat oven to 375 degrees. Spoon filling into each crepe and fold edges over. Arrange crepes in a well-greased rectangular baking dish. Spoon on white sauce, then pour on tomato sauce to cover. Bake cannelloni about 20 minutes until sauce bubbles. Serve with Parmesan cheese. *Serves six to eight*

Note: Unused crepes may be frozen and thawed for future use.

Favorite recipe from **California Brandy Advisory Board**

Stuffed Zucchini

3 lb. zucchini
1 lb. ground beef
3 tablespoons **A.1. Steak Sauce**
¼ cup chopped onion
1 clove garlic, minced
1 cup (4 oz.) shredded mild Cheddar cheese
1 jar (16 oz.) spaghetti sauce
½ cup dry bread crumbs

In boiling salted water, cook zucchini 3 minutes. Drain. Cut in half lengthwise. Scoop out seeds to form shell. Set aside. In large skillet, brown beef until crumbly. Drain. Mix in **A.1.**, onion, garlic, spaghetti sauce and ½ cheese. Fill zucchini. Arrange in 13 x 9 x 2-inch baking pan. Combine bread crumbs with remaining cheese. Sprinkle on top. Bake in preheated 350° F oven 35 minutes.

Serves 6

Zesty
Italian Meatloaf

2 cups **MALT-O-MEAL® Puffed Wheat**
2 pounds ground beef
¾ cup milk
2 eggs
1 can (8 oz.) tomato sauce
¼ cup grated Parmesan cheese
2 teaspoons dried oregano
1 teaspoon garlic salt
½ teaspoon onion salt
½ teaspoon fennel or caraway seed
½ teaspoon ground black pepper

Place Puffed Wheat in blender jar; blend at low speed until evenly crumbled. In a large bowl, mix together ground beef, crumbled Puffed Wheat, milk, eggs, about half the tomato sauce, Parmesan cheese, oregano, garlic and onion salts, fennel seed and pepper. Turn mixture into a 9 x 5-inch loaf pan. Form into an even loaf. Top with remaining tomato sauce. Bake in a 375°F oven for 1¼ hours until meat is cooked through.

Lindsay.

Mona Lindsay®'s Olive Meatloaf

2 lb. lean ground beef
1 cup chopped onions
1 clove garlic, crushed
3 bacon slices, halved
¼ tsp. pepper
½ tsp. each basil, oregano and salt
1 can (6 oz.) **LINDSAY® Pitted Black Ripe Olives**, drained
1 can (8 oz.) tomato sauce

In large bowl, thoroughly mix all ingredients except **LINDSAY® Olives**, tomato sauce and bacon. Mix in **LINDSAY® Olives**, reserving 5 for garnish. In a 9 x 13-inch baking pan, shape mixture into a 4 x 12-inch rounded loaf. Pour tomato sauce over loaf. Lay bacon slices across loaf. Bake in 350° F. oven 1 hour 15 minutes. Garnish with reserved **LINDSAY® Olives**. Slice to serve hot or cold.   *Makes 8 servings*

Meatloaf Italienne

3 tablespoons **A.1. Steak Sauce**
1 lb. ground beef
1 egg
1 teaspoon garlic salt
½ teaspoon *each* oregano and basil
¼ cup finely minced onion
1 can (8 oz.) tomato sauce
½ cup dry bread crumbs
¼ cup (1 oz.) shredded provolone cheese

Combine all ingredients except cheese. Lightly pack in 8 x 4-inch loaf pan. Bake in preheated 350° F oven 40 minutes. Top with cheese. Bake 5 minutes or until cheese is melted. Set 5 minutes. Preparation: 10 minutes. Cooking: 45 minutes.   *Serves 4*

Italian Pizza Casserole

1 can (16 oz.) **FURMAN'S® Kidney Beans**
1 can (16 oz.) **FURMAN'S® Great Northern Beans**
1 can (16 oz.) **FURMAN'S® Whole Kernel Corn**
1 lb. ground beef
1 medium onion (chopped)
½ teaspoon oregano
½ teaspoon salt
⅛ teaspoon pepper
3 cups **FURMANO'S® Pizza Sauce**
1½ cups Cheddar cheese (grated)
1 can fried onion rings

Drain beans and corn, pour in 2 quart casserole. In medium skillet brown meat over medium heat. Add onions, oregano, salt and pepper. Cook until onions are soft. Add pizza sauce, simmer 5 minutes. Stir beef mixture into beans. Bake uncovered 15 minutes. Remove from oven sprinkle with cheese and onions rings. Continue baking 15 minutes more.   *Makes 8-10 servings*

Layered Italian Casserole

2 packages **SANWA Beef Flavored Noodles RAMEN PRIDE**
½ pound ground beef
½ teaspoon salt
15½ oz. jar spaghetti sauce
1 cup cottage cheese
½ cup shredded mozzarella cheese
½ cup grated Parmesan cheese
¼ teaspoon garlic salt

Cook noodles in 4 cups boiling salted water 3 minutes. Drain. Brown beef, breaking up while cooking. Drain fat. Mix in salt, contents of seasoning packets and spaghetti sauce. Combine cottage cheese, mozzarella cheese, ¼ cup Parmesan cheese and garlic salt. In 8 inch square baking pan spread ½ cup sauce mixture. Arrange ½ of the noodles over sauce. Spread with ½ of the cheese mixture. Spoon ½ of the remaining sauce over cheese. Repeat layers. Sprinkle with remaining ¼ cup Parmesan cheese. Bake in 350° F. over 25 minutes or until heated through.
Makes about 5½ cups

Pork

Porklets Romanoff

5 porklets (pork cubed steaks)
2 tablespoons lard or drippings
1 package (5½ ounces) noodles Romanoff
2 tablespoons diced pimiento

Brown porklets on both sides in lard or drippings at moderate heat. Follow package directions for preparation of noodles Romanoff (oven method). Stir in pimiento. Arrange noodle mixture in bottom of large, shallow casserole. Arrange browned porklets on top of noodles. Cover and bake in a moderate oven (350°F.) 20 to 25 minutes.   *5 servings*

Favorite recipe from **Pork Industry Group, National Live Stock & Meat Board**

Roast Pork alla Toscana

1-4 pound loin of pork
½ clove garlic, slivered
1-8 oz. can tomato sauce
½ cup vinegar
½ cup brown sugar
¼ cup **AMARETTO from GALLIANO®**

Use small pointed knife to make deep incisions in pork; insert garlic slivers. Place pork in uncovered pan and roast at 450° for 15 to 20 minutes. Reduce heat to 350°, continue cooking pork for 2 hours or until done. While pork is cooking combine remaining ingredients in saucepan. Simmer until slightly thickened. Half an hour before roast is done, drain fat from roasting pan. Spoon about ½ of sauce over meat and baste. After 15 minutes add remaining sauce; continue basting until done.

Serves 6 to 8

Ham with Apricot Glaze
(Prosciutto Cotto con Conserva di Apricot)

1 jar (12 oz.) apricot preserves
1 tablespoon lime juice
1 teaspoon whole cloves
½ cup **LIQUORE GALLIANO®**
1-6 to 8 pound cooked ham

In small saucepan, heat apricot preserves, lime juice, cloves and **LIQUORE GALLIANO®**.

Place ham on rack in shallow roasting pan. Bake at 325° 30 minutes. Remove from oven. Remove any rind; smooth fat. Score in diamond pattern, if desired. Return to oven. Bake 1½ hours longer, basting or brushing frequently with apricot glaze.

Serves 8-10

Italian Melt

2 slices (1 oz.) part-skim mozzarella cheese, divided
2 slices thin sliced diet bread
2 slices (2 oz.) **KAHN'S® Cooked Ham**
1 slice tomato, thinly sliced
Dash oregano
1 egg

Place 1 slice of cheese on one slice of bread. Add ham and tomato and season with oregano. Top with remaining slice of cheese and bread. In small bowl, mix egg with a few drops of water. Dip assembled sandwich into egg, turning, so that egg is absorbed into bread. Spray a nonstick skillet with nonstick cooking spray; heat over medium heat. Add the sandwich and cook, turning occasionally, until both sides are browned and cheese is melted.

Makes 1 serving

Calories: 300 calories per serving

Sausage

Tuscany Sausage Skillet

8 sweet Italian sausages (about 1 lb.) sliced
⅓ cup water
1 package (10 oz.) **BIRDS EYE® Italian Style Vegetables with a Seasoned Sauce**

Brown sausages well in skillet. Add water and simmer 5 minutes. Move sausages to one side of skillet. Add vegetables. Bring to a *full* boil over medium heat, separate vegetables with a fork; stir frequently. Reduce heat; cover and simmer for 2 minutes.

Makes about 3½ cups or 3 servings

Italian Sausage Loaf

1 (one pound) loaf **BRIDGFORD Frozen Bread Dough**
4 hot Italian sausage
4 sweet Italian sausage
1 medium green pepper, sliced
1 medium onion, chopped
½ cup spaghetti sauce
3 oz. mozzarella cheese, grated
2 Tbsp. Parmesan cheese, grated
2 Tbsp. butter, melted

Let dough thaw to room temperature. Cook whole sausages thoroughly. Drain well and reserve 2 Tbsp. fat. Split in half lengthwise. Sauté green pepper and onion in fat until tender.

On lightly floured board roll dough out to 15 inch x 9 inch rectangle. Fold ⅓ of dough over middle to make a 10 inch x 9 inch rectangle. Arrange cut sausage on folded dough. Spread green pepper, onions, and spaghetti sauce respectively over sausage. Sprinkle with grated mozzarella cheese. Fold remaining ⅓ of dough over sausage filling; seal all edges tightly. Place on lightly greased sheet pan. Brush dough with melted butter; sprinkle with Parmesan cheese. Let rise 30 minutes. Bake in preheated 350° oven for 30-35 minutes or until golden brown. Slice and serve.

Serves 4-6

Antipasto Sandwich

1 package (8 oz.) **OSCAR MAYER Hard Salami**
1 loaf (1 lb.) unsliced bread, about 10-inches long
1 head lettuce
6 to 8 oz. provolone or mozzarella cheese, sliced thin or cut into bite-size pieces
24 ripe olives
2 tomatoes, cut into wedges
Pickled mild Italian peppers
Italian salad dressing

Slice bread lengthwise into four flat pieces. Top each slice with lettuce. Arrange salami, cheese and olives on top. Garnish with tomato wedges and peppers. Serve with Italian salad dressing.

Makes four open-faced servings

Skillet Supper Italiano

1 lb. **HILLSHIRE FARM® Smoked Sausage**, cut into ½ inch pieces
3 Tbsp. chopped onion
½ cup chopped green pepper
10½ oz. can pizza sauce
1 Tbsp. Worcestershire sauce
1½ tsp. salt
1½ cups cooked macaroni
Grated Parmesan or mozzarella cheese

Sauté sausage, onion and green pepper until onions and peppers are tender. Mix in pizza sauce, Worcestershire sauce, salt and cooked macaroni. Simmer, covered, for 8-10 minutes or until heated through. Serve with grated cheese.

Yield: 4 servings

Cheese Polenta & Sausage Casserole

1 8⅛ oz. package corn muffin mix
½ cup **MERKT'S Cheese,** any flavor
1 Tbsp. butter
1 lb. sweet Italian sausage links
1 large onion, chopped
1 garlic clove, chopped
1 1-lb. can whole tomatoes, drained & chopped
  (reserve ½ cup liquid)
3-oz. tomato paste
½ tsp. oregano
Salt & pepper
¾ cup **MERKT'S Cheese**

Grease 2-quart baking dish. Prepare corn muffin mix according to package directions, add ½ cup **MERKT'S Cheese** to batter. Turn into prepared dish, spreading evenly. Set mixture aside.

Preheat oven to 375°F. Heat butter in skillet over medium heat. Add sausage & cook, turning frequently, until browned on all sides, about 15 min. Slice sausage in half lengthwise & set aside. Add onion & garlic to skillet. Increase heat & sauté until tender, about 7-10 min. Add tomatoes & liquid, tomato paste, oregano, salt & pepper & continue cooking until sauce is thickened, about 5 min. Arrange half of sausage over corn muffin batter. Spread tomato sauce over evenly. Top with remaining sausage. Bake 15 min. Top with remaining cheese & continue baking until cheese melts, about 10 min. Serve hot.

Easy Italian Casserole

1 lb. pork sausage
1 lb. ground beef
1 cup chopped onion
1 teaspoon Italian Seasoning
½ teaspoon garlic powder
1 (29½ oz.) can **HUNT'S® MANWICH® Sloppy Joe Sauce**
1 cup water
1 (16-oz.) pkg. shell macaroni, cooked and drained
2 cups grated mozzarella cheese
½ cup grated Parmesan cheese

In a large skillet, cook pork and beef until it loses redness; drain fat. Add onion, Italian seasoning and garlic powder; cook until onion is soft. Add **MANWICH®** and water; simmer 5 minutes. In a 3-quart casserole, layer *half* the meat mixture, macaroni and both cheeses. Repeat layers using *remaining* meat, macaroni, and cheeses. Bake at 350° F 30 minutes.   *Makes 6 to 8 servings*

Veal & Lamb

Lamb Italiano

¼ cup butter or margarine
2 Tbsp. Worcestershire sauce
1 tsp. garlic powder
2 tsp. **BALTIMORE SPICE OLD BAY Seasoning**
4 lamb chops or 2 pounds boneless/shoulder
Green pepper slices

Heat oven to 450°. Arrange lamb chops on broiler pan. Combine remaining ingredients except green pepper and brush onto meat. Garnish with green pepper slices. Roast 30 minutes for chops and 45 minutes for shoulder.   *4 servings*

Veal Parmesan

⅓ cup flour
1 teaspoon salt
1 teaspoon dry parsley flakes
1 teaspoon basil
¼ teaspoon pepper
¼ cup grated Parmesan cheese
2 pounds veal cutlet, cut ½-inch thick
1 egg
1 tablespoon water
½ cup **PURITAN® Oil**
2 tablespoons chopped onion
1 cup (8-oz.) can tomato sauce
⅓ cup (4-oz. can) sliced mushrooms
¼ cup sherry, if desired

Mix first six ingredients and place in large plastic or paper bag. Cut veal into serving pieces, dip in egg beaten with water, then shake in bag with flour mixture. Brown meat on both sides in hot **PURITAN® Oil** in a heavy skillet. Remove meat. Add onion, tomato sauce, mushrooms and any remaining flour mixture to skillet. Stir until mixture bubbles. Add meat; cover and cook over low heat for about 45 minutes, until meat is tender. Stir in sherry, if desired.   *4-5 servings*

Veal Scallopini

2 pounds veal round, sliced ½-inch thick
LAWRY'S® Seasoned Salt, to taste
LAWRY'S® Seasoned Pepper, to taste
Flour
½ cup butter
½ pound fresh mushrooms, sliced
1 large onion
1 sprig fresh parsley
¼ teaspoon each: rosemary and oregano
½ teaspoon **LAWRY'S® Seasoned Salt**
¼ teaspoon **LAWRY'S® Seasoned Pepper**
1 cup dry white wine
1 tablespoon sugar

Sprinkle meat with Seasoned Salt and Seasoned Pepper; dredge in flour. Melt ¼ cup of butter in large skillet and brown meat slowly on both sides; remove to platter and keep warm. Sauté mushrooms in 2 tablespoons of butter until just golden; remove from pan and set aside. Finely chop together onion and parsley, add rosemary and oregano; sauté in remaining 2 tablespoons of butter until onion is golden brown. Add mushrooms, Seasoned Salt, Seasoned Pepper, wine and sugar; cook just until heated through. Spoon over meat and serve immediately. *Makes 6 to 8 servings*

PROVIMI VEAL

Veal Paprika

1 pkg. (12 oz.) **DELFT BLUE®-PROVIMI® Fancy Veal Slices,** thawed but cold
3 Tbsp. butter
2 Tbsp. oil
2 medium onions, sliced
1 red pepper, seeded, chopped
2 Tbsp. flour
1⅔ cups whipping cream
1 tsp. chicken stock base
½ tsp. sweet paprika
⅓ cup grated Gruyère or Swiss cheese
3 Tbsp. grated Parmesan cheese
1½ cups frozen peas, cooked, drained
⅓ cup dairy sour cream
Salt and white pepper to taste
6 oz. medium noodles, cooked, drained

Prepare veal slices according to BASIC DIRECTIONS.* Remove from pan; keep warm. In drippings, sauté onion and pepper until onion is limp over medium heat. Stir in flour; cook until bubbly. Gradually add cream, cooking and stirring until thickened and bubbly. Stir in stock base, paprika, cheeses and peas. Stir until cheeses are melted. Stir in sour cream; taste and adjust seasonings. Combine half of sauce with noodles in serving dish; arrange veal on top. Serve with remaining sauce.   *Makes 4 to 6 servings*

*BASIC DIRECTIONS:
Thaw slices 30 minutes. Remove from package; place each slice between 2 sheets of waxed-paper. Pound with flat side of mallet to about ¹⁄₁₆ inch thickness. Sprinkle both sides of meat with salt, pepper and flour. Heat 3 Tbsp. butter and 2 Tbsp. oil in large skillet. Sauté over medium heat 1½ to 2 minutes per side.

Ossobuco Milanese

4 pounds veal shank bones, cut into thirds
Flour
3 tablespoons oil
1 onion, chopped
1 carrot, chopped
1 stalk celery, chopped
1 clove garlic
1 teaspoon dried marjoram
1 small piece lemon rind
Salt and pepper
½ cup dry white wine
4 ripe tomatoes
1½ cups brown veal stock
1 clove crushed garlic
1 teaspoon grated orange rind
1 teaspoon lemon rind

Brown shank bones dusted with flour in oil. Brown all sides. Add chopped onion, carrot and celery, garlic, marjoram and lemon rind, salt and pepper. Stir for two minutes, add white wine and cook until evaporated. Place veal bones upright so marrow does not fall out. Add tomatoes and stock; add more stock as needed. Bring to boil and cover pot. Simmer 1 hour. Remove lid and add rest of ingredients; simmer, stirring occasionally until meat is tender.   *Serves 6-8*

Favorite recipe from **Cling Peach Advisory Board**

Veal Cutlet Parmesan

1 lb. veal cutlets
½ lb. mozzarella cheese
1 cup dry breadcrumbs
2 beaten eggs
1 can tomato sauce
1 tsp. salt
Dash of pepper

Dip cutlets in beaten eggs combined with seasoning, then in mixture of Parmesan cheese and breadcrumbs. Fry in **FILIPPO BERIO Olive Oil** until brown (about 8 minutes). Then place cutlets in baking dish, spread tomato sauce and slices of mozzarella cheese over them.

Bake in moderate oven 10 to 15 minutes.   *Serves 4*

Veal Florentine Style
(Vitello alla Fiorentina)

1 small onion, sliced
¼ cup olive oil
2 pound veal rump, cubed
1 clove garlic
1 cup canned tomato puree
Pinch of rosemary
¼ cup **SAMBUCA from GALLIANO®**
Salt and pepper to taste

Fry onion in oil for 2 minutes. Add garlic and brown 1 minute longer. Add meat and brown well on all sides over medium heat. Add remaining ingredients, cover pan, and cook over low heat until meat is tender, about 30 minutes. Stir occasionally. Serve hot over rice or polenta.   *Serves 4*

Holland House®

Veal Bolognese

6 large slices of veal cut about ¼ inch thick
Freshly ground black pepper
2 egg yolks
1 cup breadcrumbs
Butter
6 thin slices prosciutto
6 slices Gruyère cheese
½ cup **HOLLAND HOUSE® Sherry Cooking Wine**
Parsley sprigs

On a cutting board pound veal cutlets with a meat mallet or the side of a cleaver until they are about ⅛ inch thick. Dry veal with paper towels, sprinkle with freshly ground pepper. Dip in beaten egg yolks, cover them thoroughly with breadcrumbs. In a skillet melt enough butter to cover the bottom of pan. Brown veal cutlets over fairly high heat (no more than 3 minutes on each side). Remove from skillet and place in baking dish. Cover each cutlet with slices of prosciutto and Gruyère. Add Sherry to skillet and deglaze, scraping the pan to loosen any brown bits of breadcrumbs which may adhere to the bottom and sides. Pour contents of skillet over veal in baking dish and place in a preheated 350° oven. Bake for about 5 minutes or until cheese is melted. Remove from oven and garnish with parsley sprigs.   *Makes 6 servings*

Veal Mozzarella

2 eggs
2 Tbsp. **FALBO'S Romano** or **Parmesan**
½ tsp. salt
¼ tsp. pepper
1 Tbsp. chopped parsley
4 slices veal 4 in. by ¼ in.
⅓ cup olive oil
½ recipe Plain Tomato Sauce* (recipe follows)
⅓ lb. **FALBO'S Mozzarella** or **Scamorza,** sliced ¼ in. thick

Beat eggs, add grated cheese, salt, pepper and parsley. Dip veal in batter then roll in bread crumbs. Chill for 20 min. or longer to make browning easier. Heat oil in a skillet and reduce heat to medium. Brown breaded veal on both sides, remove and place in a shallow baking dish. Pour on ⅔ of the tomato sauce, put sliced Mozzarella on and spread rest of sauce on top. Bake in a preheated 350 degree oven for 15-20 minutes. Serve while still hot.

Yield: 4 servings

*The other half may be used on a spaghetti side dish traditionally served with the veal.

Note: Eggplant can be substituted for veal.

Plain Tomato Sauce

3 Tbsp. olive or cooking oil
1 small onion chopped
16 oz. can tomato paste
3 cups water
1 large can (2½) plum tomatoes (strained)
½ tsp. crushed basil
½ tsp. oregano
Salt and pepper to taste

Simmer onion in oil until soft. Add tomato paste, water and tomatoes and blend. Add basil and oregano, stir and cook on low heat for about an hour. Add salt and pepper.

Yield: 6-7 cups sauce

Poultry

wesson® oil

Chicken Italienne

3 lb. frying chicken pieces
3 Tbsp. **WESSON® Oil**
¾ cup water
1 (6-oz.) can **HUNT'S® Tomato Paste**
1 (4-oz.) can button mushrooms, undrained
1 clove garlic, crushed
1 cup chicken broth
⅓ cup minced onion
¼ cup dry red wine
2 Tbsp. minced parsley
1 tsp. Italian herb seasoning
½ tsp. sugar
8 oz. spinach or egg noodles, cooked and drained
2 Tbsp. flour

Brown chicken in oil in 12-inch skillet; drain fat. Combine ½ cup water and remaining ingredients *except* noodles and flour; mix well. Pour over chicken. Cover; simmer 30 minutes. Arrange chicken on noodles on warm platter. Combine remaining water and flour and use to thicken skillet juices. Serve with chicken and noodles.
Makes 4 to 6 servings

Heinz Chicken Parmesan

2 to 2½ pounds broiler-fryer pieces
¼ cup all-purpose flour
1¼ teaspoons salt
¼ teaspoon pepper
3 tablespoons shortening
1 can (1 pound) tomatoes, cut into bite-size pieces
⅓ cup **HEINZ 57 Sauce**
⅓ cup grated Parmesan cheese
1 tablespoon granulated sugar
¼ teaspoon oregano leaves, crushed
¼ pound sliced mozzarella cheese, cut into strips*
Hot buttered noodles

Coat chicken with mixture of flour, salt and pepper; brown well in shortening. Place chicken in baking dish (12x7½x2 inch). Blend any remaining flour mixture with tomatoes and next 4 ingredients; pour over chicken. Cover; bake in 350°F. oven, 30 minutes. Remove cover; top with mozzarella cheese. Bake, uncovered, an additional 25-30 minutes or until chicken is tender. Skim excess fat from sauce. Serve sauce over chicken and noodles.
Makes 4-5 servings (about 2 cups sauce)

*1 cup shredded mozzarella cheese may be substituted.

Smoked Chicken Florentine Pie

1 cup buttermilk biscuit mix
¼ cup milk
2 eggs, beaten
¼ cup chopped green onion
2 2½ oz. packages **BUDDIG Smoked Sliced Chicken**
1 package (10 oz.) frozen chopped spinach, thawed and drained
1 cup shredded Muenster cheese
1 carton (12 oz.) cottage cheese
½ teaspoon salt
½ teaspoon ground nutmeg
¼ teaspoon white pepper
2 cloves garlic, minced
2 eggs, beaten
⅓ cup grated Parmesan cheese

Combine together until smooth, biscuit mix, milk, 2 eggs and green onion. Spread over bottom of greased 12 x 8-inch baking dish. Place **BUDDIG Chicken** slices over batter. Combine spinach, cheeses, seasonings, garlic and 2 eggs. Spoon over chicken. Sprinkle Parmesan cheese over top. Bake in 375° F. oven for 30 minutes or until dough is baked and filling is set. Let stand 5 minutes before serving.
Serves 6 to 8
(Continued)

MICROWAVE METHOD:

Beat together until smooth the biscuit mix, milk, 2 eggs and green onion. Spread over bottom of greased 12 x 8 inch glass dish. Cook on high for 3 to 4 minutes, rotating dish ½ turn once. Lay **BUDDIG Chicken** slices over dough. Combine spinach, cheeses, seasonings, garlic and 2 eggs; spoon over chicken. Sprinkle Parmesan cheese over top. Cook on high for 5 to 7 minutes, rotating dish ½ turn after 3 minutes. Let stand 5 minutes before serving.

Serves 6 to 8

Chicken Thighs Parmigiana

(Microwave Recipe)

6 **COUNTRY PRIDE®** Broiler-fryer Chicken Thighs, boned and skinned
1 egg, beaten
¼ cup water
1 cup fine dry bread crumbs
3 tablespoons butter or margarine
2 cans (8 oz. each) tomato sauce
1 clove garlic, minced
½ teaspoon salt
½ teaspoon dried leaf basil
½ teaspoon dried leaf oregano
¼ cup grated Parmesan cheese
4 oz. mozzarella cheese, cut into 6 slices

Flatten chicken thighs by pounding between two pieces of waxed paper. Beat egg with ¼ cup water in small shallow dish. Dip chicken thighs in egg, then in bread crumbs. In 12 x 7½ x 2-inch glass baking dish melt butter in microwave oven 1 minute. Place thighs top side down in dish. Cook in microwave oven 10 minutes. Turn thighs over and turn dish. Cook 10 minutes longer. Mix tomato sauce, garlic, salt, basil and oregano; pour over chicken and cover with waxed paper. Cook 5 minutes. Turn dish, uncover, sprinkle with Parmesan cheese, and place a cheese slice on each chicken thigh. Cook 2 to 5 minutes, until chicken is tender and cheese melts. Let stand 3 to 5 minutes before serving. Total cooking time: 30 minutes.

Yield: 6 servings

Chicken Italiano

3 whole chicken breasts, halved and skinned
2 cans (6 ounces each) tomato sauce
2 medium-size carrots, thinly sliced
¼ cup (½ medium-size) diced onion
½ cup green pepper seeded and diced
2 tablespoons lemon juice
1 clove garlic, crushed
½ teaspoon basil
¼ teaspoon oregano
¼ teaspoon salt
Freshly ground pepper to taste
½ pound mushrooms, sliced
1 packet **SWEET 'N LOW®**

Brown chicken in large non-stick saucepan. Add remaining ingredients, except mushrooms and **SWEET 'N LOW®**. Cover and simmer 30 minutes. Add mushrooms and cook, uncovered, 10 to 15 minutes, or until chicken is tender. Stir in **SWEET 'N LOW®**.

6 servings

PER SERVING (½ chicken breast):
Calories: 215   Protein: 31gm
Carbohydrate: 10gm   Fat: 4gm
                       Sodium: 565mg

Banquet® Chicken Italian

1 package (2 lb.) **BANQUET®** Heat and Serve Frozen Fully Cooked Fried Chicken
1 small onion, sliced (about ¼ cup)
2 tablespoons butter or margarine, melted
2 tablespoons flour
2 cans (16 oz. each) stewed tomatoes
1 cup (8 oz.) dairy sour cream
½ cup grated Parmesan cheese, divided

Place chicken in 3-quart oblong baking dish. Heat in 375°F oven 25 minutes. Meanwhile, in small saucepan sauté onion in butter until tender. Stir in flour; add tomatoes. Heat to boiling. Pour tomato mixture over hot chicken. In small bowl, combine sour cream and ¼ cup cheese. Spoon on top of chicken pieces. Sprinkle remaining ¼ cup cheese on top. Heat an additional 20 to 25 minutes or until hot.

Makes 5 servings

Chicken Breasts Romano

3 whole chicken breasts, split in half
3 tablespoons seasoned flour
¼ cup shortening
¼ cup onion, finely chopped
2 cups **LIBBY'S®** Tomato Juice
2 tablespoons Romano cheese
1 tablespoon sugar
½ teaspoon salt
½ teaspoon garlic salt
½ teaspoon oregano
¼ teaspoon basil
1 teaspoon vinegar
1 can (3-oz.) sliced mushrooms
1 tablespoon fresh parsley, minced
1 cup shredded American or Cheddar cheese

Shake chicken breasts in a bag with salt and pepper seasoned flour to coat evenly. In large skillet brown the chicken in the shortening. Remove chicken from skillet. Discard all but 1 tablespoon shortening. Add onions and lightly brown. Add tomato juice which has been combined with Romano cheese, sugar, salt, garlic salt, oregano, basil, vinegar, mushrooms and parsley. Cover and simmer 45 minutes or until chicken is tender and sauce is the consistency of gravy. Sprinkle with shredded cheese before serving.

Yields 6 servings

Chicken Roma

1 broiler-fryer chicken (2½ to 3 pounds), cut into
    pieces
4 cups **KELLOGG'S CORN FLAKES®** Cereal,
    crushed into fine crumbs
1 teaspoon salt
¼ teaspoon pepper
2 tablespoons chopped parsley
½ teaspoon crushed oregano
1 clove garlic, crushed
½ cup light cream or undiluted evaporated milk
Fresh lemon wedges

Wash chicken pieces and dry thoroughly. Combine finely crushed
CORN FLAKES® Cereal, salt, pepper, parsley, oregano and
garlic. Dip chicken pieces into cream or undiluted evaporated
milk, then roll in seasoned **CORN FLAKES®** Cereal crumbs
until evenly coated. Place chicken pieces skin side up in a single
layer in a well-greased shallow baking pan; do not crowd pieces.
Bake in preheated oven (350° F.) about 1 hour, or until drumstick
is tender when pierced with a fork. No need to cover pan or turn
chicken while cooking. Serve with fresh lemon, if desired.

Makes 4 to 5 servings

® Kellogg Company

The Gladiator

4 hard rolls, split
Spinach leaves
½ pound **WEAVER®** Sliced White Meat Chicken
    Roll
4 slices (4 oz.) provolone cheese
8 slices (4 oz.) hard salami
4 green pepper rings
¼ cup creamy Italian dressing

On rolls, layer spinach, chicken, cheese, salami and pepper.
Drizzle with dressing.   *4 servings*

Chicken Parmesan

¼ cup milk
1 egg, slightly beaten
⅓ cup grated Parmesan cheese
⅓ cup dry bread crumbs
2 whole chicken breasts, skinned, boned and halved
    lengthwise
2 tablespoons vegetable oil
1 jar **LA SAUCE®** Chicken Baking Sauce—Italian
    Style
⅓ cup water
¼ cup sherry
½ cup (2 oz.) shredded mozzarella cheese
Hot cooked spaghetti

In small bowl, combine milk and egg. In another bowl, mix
Parmesan cheese and bread crumbs. Dip chicken in milk and egg;
roll in Parmesan cheese and bread crumbs. In large fry pan, brown
chicken in oil on medium heat on both sides 8 minutes. Remove
chicken from pan. Combine **LA SAUCE®**, water and sherry; stir
into pan drippings. Place chicken pieces on top of sauce. Simmer,
covered, on low heat 25 minutes. Sprinkle mozzarella cheese on
chicken pieces; simmer, covered, 5 minutes. Serve on spaghetti.

4 servings

Easy
Chicken Cacciatore

2 medium onions, sliced
2 cloves garlic, minced
2 Tbsp. olive oil
1 2½-3 lb. broiler-fryer chicken, cut up
1 16 oz. can **S&W®** Italian Style Stewed Tomatoes
1 8 oz. can **S&W®** Tomato Sauce
1 2½ oz. jar whole mushrooms, drained
1 tsp. salt
¼ tsp. pepper
¼ cup dry white wine
Hot cooked rice

In a large skillet, sauté onions and garlic in oil over medium heat
till onions are tender. Remove onions; set aside. In same skillet,
brown chicken pieces over medium heat about 15 minutes, turning
to brown evenly. Add more oil to the skillet if needed. Return
onions to skillet. Combine undrained Italian Style Stewed
Tomatoes, tomato sauce, mushrooms, salt and pepper. Pour over
chicken in skillet. Cover and simmer for 30 minutes. Stir in wine.
Cook, uncovered, over low heat about 10-15 minutes longer or till
chicken is tender, turning occasionally. Serve over rice.

Serves 4

Chicken Cacciatore

¼ cup flour
1 teaspoon seasoned salt
1 teaspoon paprika
⅛ teaspoon black pepper
6 chicken legs and thighs, connected
¼ cup oil
1 can (1 lb.) **STOKELY'S FINEST®** Tomatoes
1 can (8 oz.) **STOKELY'S FINEST®** Tomato Sauce
½ cup onion, chopped
½ cup green pepper, chopped
½ cup white wine
1 clove garlic, minced
1 teaspoon Italian seasoning
¼ teaspoon ground thyme
½ lb. medium wide noodles, cooked

Combine first 4 ingredients and coat chicken. In skillet, brown
chicken in oil; drain. Add next 8 ingredients. Cover and simmer
slowly for 1 hour, or until chicken is tender. Serve over noodles.

Makes 6 servings

La Sauce® Chicken Cacciatore

1 2½ to 3-lb. chicken, cut up
2 tablespoons vegetable oil
1 jar LA SAUCE® Chicken Baking Sauce—Italian Style
¼ cup dry white wine
1 tablespoon sugar, if desired
Hot cooked spaghetti

In large fry pan, brown chicken in oil on medium heat 15 minutes. Remove chicken from skillet; reserve drippings. In same skillet, combine ⅓ cup reserved drippings, LA SAUCE®, wine and sugar; place chicken pieces on top. Simmer, covered, on low heat 30 minutes, stirring occasionally. Serve on spaghetti.   *4 servings*

Turkey Italiano with Vegetables

1 package (2 to 3 lb.) LOUIS RICH™ Fresh Turkey Drumsticks
1 can (16 oz.) stewed tomatoes
1 teaspoon Italian herb seasoning*
⅛ teaspoon garlic powder
1 bag (1 lb.) frozen vegetable blend
2 tablespoons cornstarch
2 tablespoons grated Parmesan cheese

Rinse turkey and pat dry. Place drumsticks in 3 quart casserole or Dutch oven. Add tomatoes, herbs and garlic. Bake, covered, in 350°F oven 1½ hours. Add vegetables. Cover and bake ½ hour more. Remove meat, cover to keep warm. Add a small amount of hot liquid to cornstarch to form paste; mix well. Add cornstarch; cook and stir over medium heat until thickened. Arrange on platter with turkey. Sprinkle with cheese. Serve with spaghetti squash, if desired.   *Makes 4 servings, 355 calories each (without squash)*

*Note: ¾ teaspoon oregano and ¼ teaspoon basil may be substituted for the Italian herb seasoning.

Turkey alla Parmigiana

1 pound raw turkey breast, sliced ½-inch thick
¾ teaspoon AC′CENT® Flavor Enhancer, divided
1 egg
4 tablespoons vegetable oil, divided
½ cup seasoned bread crumbs
1 small onion, chopped
2 cloves garlic, minced
2 cans (8 ounces each) tomato sauce
½ teaspoon dried leaf basil
¼ teaspoon dried leaf oregano
⅛ teaspoon pepper
1 cup (4 ounces) shredded mozzarella cheese

Sprinkle ½ teaspoon AC′CENT® on turkey slices. In small bowl beat egg with 3 tablespoons oil. Dip turkey in egg mixture. Coat in bread crumbs. Arrange in 1½ quart baking dish. Bake in a 450°F. oven 30 minutes. In small saucepan heat remaining 1 tablespoon oil; sauté onion and garlic. Add tomato sauce, remaining ¼ teaspoon AC′CENT®, basil, oregano and pepper. Simmer 20 minutes. Pour sauce over turkey slices. Sprinkle with mozzarella cheese. Return to oven. Bake 10 minutes longer or until cheese is melted.   *Yield: 4 servings*

Tacchino Tonnato

1 5-pound turkey breast
3 cans (13¾ ounces each) chicken broth
2 cups dry white wine
2 cups water
2 onions, quartered
2 carrots, pared and cut in quarters
2 ribs celery with leaves, cut in chunks
2 bay leaves
6 sprigs parsley
2 whole cloves
¼ teaspoon TABASCO® Pepper Sauce

In large kettle place turkey breast and add remaining ingredients. Cover and simmer 1 hour and 40 minutes, or until turkey is tender. Remove from heat, and cool in refrigerator in stock. When cold, remove turkey from stock and cut into slices. Reserve ⅓ cup stock and prepare Tonnato Sauce.* Spread a little sauce over bottom of a 13 x 9 x 2-inch baking dish. Arrange turkey slices over sauce and cover with remaining sauce. Cover and refrigerate overnight. To serve, let stand at room temperature 30 minutes. Arrange on platter and garnish with lemon slices, sliced pitted black olives, sliced scallions and watercress. Serve with marinated tomatoes and Italian bread.   *Yield: 6 to 8 servings*

*Tonnato Sauce

¾ cup olive oil
2 egg yolks
1 can (6½ or 7 ounces) tuna, drained
½ teaspoon salt
6 anchovy fillets, rinsed and chopped
3 tablespoons lemon juice
⅓ cup reserved turkey stock
½ teaspoon TABASCO® Pepper Sauce
¼ cup heavy cream
2 tablespoons capers, rinsed and drained

In container of electric blender, combine olive oil, egg yolks, tuna, salt, anchovy fillets, lemon juice, reserved turkey stock and TABASCO® Sauce. Cover and process at high speed until smooth. Pour into a bowl; stir in heavy cream and capers.

Roaster Marinara

1 PERDUE® Oven Stuffer Roaster (5-7 pounds)
½ teaspoon basil, crushed
Salt and pepper
1½ cups marinara sauce
1 package (6 oz.) sliced mozzarella cheese

Preheat oven to 350°F. Remove giblets from roaster. Season with basil, salt and pepper. Check to see that Bird-Watcher Thermometer is flush against breast. It will pop out when roaster is done, (approximately 1¾ to 2¼ hours for 5 to 6 pound bird, and 2 to 2½ hours for 6 to 7 pound bird). Place bird, breast side up, in roasting pan. Brush 1½ cups marinara sauce over roaster 30 minutes before roaster is done. Cut mozzarella cheese into long strips ½ inch wide and place in lattice pattern over breast, during final 10 minutes of cooking.

Cornish Italiano

2-3 **TYSON® Cornish Game Hens** (halved)
1½ tsp. sage
1 tsp. rosemary
1 tsp. garlic powder
1 tsp. salt
⅛ tsp. pepper
2 Tbsp. butter
2 Tbsp. olive oil
1 cup dry white wine
1 Tbsp. flour

Mix dry seasonings and rub game hens inside and out. In Dutch oven melt butter and oil and brown hens on all sides. Add wine, cover and simmer until tender (approximately 45 minutes). Remove hens to platter, cover and keep warm.

Mix flour with ½ cup warm water and add to pan juices for Cornish sauce. Serve with noodles mixed with sour cream and Parmesan cheese.

Seafood

Rainbow Trout Italiano

Pour **WISH-BONE® Italian Dressing** in a dish with **CLEAR SPRINGS Rainbow Trout** and let marinate for two hours or more. Remove the trout and broil or cook as you would otherwise.

Halibut Steaks, Italiano

4 halibut steaks (about 2 pounds) 1-inch thick
6 tablespoons salad oil
½ cup water
1 chicken bouillon cube
1 tablespoon fresh grated **SUNKIST® Lemon** peel
2 tablespoons fresh squeezed **SUNKIST® Lemon** juice
¼ teaspoon tarragon leaves, crushed
½ teaspoon salt
¼ cup chopped onion
2 tablespoons raisins
2 tablespoons sliced almonds
SUNKIST® Lemon wedges

In skillet, lightly brown steaks in oil; pour off fat. Add remaining ingredients except almonds and lemon wedges. Cook, covered, over low heat 5 minutes or until fish flakes easily. Sprinkle with almonds. Serve with lemon wedges. *Makes 4 servings*

Fish-Eggplant Parmigiana

1-14 oz. pkg. **HIGH LINER® Fillets**, thawed
1 large eggplant
2-3 eggs, beaten
1½-2 cups dry, fine bread crumbs
1-14 oz. can tomato sauce
Oregano, garlic salt, basil
8 oz. mozzarella cheese, shredded
Grated Parmesan cheese

Slice eggplant into ½ inch slices. Dip in egg and then in bread crumbs. Brown in ¼ cup hot oil on both sides. Arrange slices on bottom of a shallow baking dish. Place fish on top of eggplant. Pour tomato sauce over all and sprinkle lightly with oregano, garlic salt and basil. Top with mozzarella and Parmesan cheese. Bake in 350° F oven 30-40 minutes. *Serves 3-4*

Pizza Fish Sticks

1 32 oz. package **FISHER BOY® Fish Sticks**
1 15 oz. can tomato sauce
1 8 oz. package shredded mozzarella cheese
Grated Parmesan cheese

Preheat oven to 425°F. Place 16 fish sticks in greased baking dish. Cover with ½ can tomato sauce. Sprinkle with ½ package shredded mozzarella cheese. Top with grated Parmesan cheese. Repeat layers with remaining fish sticks, tomato sauce and cheeses. Bake for 25-30 minutes. Recipe may be cut in half.

Cioppino

1 lb. firm fleshed fish (cod, turbot, haddock, etc.) and/or seafood (raw shrimp, scallops, steamed clams)
2 Tbsp. butter or margarine
1 large onion, 1-inch diced
1 large green pepper, 1-inch diced
2 cloves garlic, finely chopped
1 cup water
1 1 lb. can tomatoes, chopped, plus their juice
1 Tbsp. **BALTIMORE SPICE OLD BAY Seasoning**
¼ tsp. basil
¼ tsp. marjoram
¾ cup red wine
6 or more mushrooms, halved

Cut deboned fish in large bite-size pieces. Sauté vegetables in butter until crisp-tender. Add water, tomatoes with juice, and seasonings; heat to boiling. Reduce heat, cover and simmer 10 minutes. Add wine and mushrooms; bring to boiling. Reduce heat, cover and simmer 10 minutes. Add fish, shrimp and/or scallops, cover and simmer until done, about 8 minutes. Clams (if used) should be added during last 3 minutes.

Welch's

Scallops in Shells

1½ pounds scallops
Butter
6 green onions, chopped
Bouquet garni (parsley, celery, thyme & bay leaf)
1½ cups **WELCH'S® White Grape Juice**
¼ pound mushrooms, chopped
3 tablespoons flour
Salt and pepper
1 cup light cream
Parmesan cheese
Bread crumbs

Dry scallops on paper towel. Place in saucepan with 2 tablespoons butter, onion and bouquet garni. Cover with white grape juice. Bring to a boil, reduce heat and simmer for about 4 minutes or until scallops are just tender. Drain and reserve broth. Cut scallops into small pieces or slices. Sauté mushrooms in 2 tablespoons butter. Blend in flour, salt and pepper. Stir in cream and ½ cup broth. Cook and stir until thickened. Add scallops. Spoon into individual shells. Sprinkle with Parmesan cheese and crumbs. Just before serving, brown lightly under broiler.   *Makes 6 servings*

Lobster Fra Diavolo

2 lb. **ATALANTA Frozen Lobster Tails**, thawed
½ cup olive oil
4 Tbsp. parsley, chopped
1 tsp. oregano, dried
½ tsp. basil, dried
⅛ tsp. salt
Pepper as needed
1 cup onion, chopped
1 clove garlic, minced
2 cups canned tomatoes
2 Tbsp. cognac

Heat the olive oil and add lobster. (Remove membrane and cut tails in sections.) Toss well until shells are red. Add parsley, oregano, basil, salt and pepper and simmer for ten minutes. Then add onion, garlic and tomatoes. Stir and cover. Cook for 20 minutes. Add cognac. Serve over rice.   *Yield: 6 servings*

Mediterranean Fillets

1 package **VAN DE KAMP'S® Today's Catch Cod** or **Fish Fillets**
1 medium onion, thinly sliced
½ green pepper, or more to taste, thinly sliced
1 Tbsp. olive oil
1 clove garlic, crushed
¼ tsp. each salt and thyme
⅛ tsp. each pepper and oregano
¼ cup dry white wine or chicken stock
1 Tbsp. tomato paste
2 Tbsp. chopped parsley

Preheat oven to 425°. Place fillets in lightly oiled casserole. Arrange onions and pepper slices over fish. Combine remaining ingredients except parsley and pour over fish. Bake 25 minutes, spooning some of sauce over fish halfway through cooking. Garnish with chopped parsley.

MICROWAVE METHOD:
In 8-inch square microwave-safe dish, combine onions, peppers, garlic and oil, then microwave on HIGH 2 minutes. Combine remaining ingredients except parsley in glass measuring cup. Microwave on HIGH 1 minute. Slide fillets under cooked vegetables, then pour tomato mixture over all. Microwave on HIGH 10 minutes, rotating dish twice during cooking. Garnish with parsley.   *Serves 2*

Calories: 143 calories per serving.

Rock Lobster Mariscada

4 pkgs. (9 oz. ea.) **SOUTH AFRICAN ROCK LOBSTER Tails,** thawed
½ cup olive oil
2 garlic cloves, minced
6 scallions, chopped
2 tablespoons minced Italian parsley
2 tablespoons flour
1 tablespoon monosodium glutamate
2 eggs
1 cup light cream
1 cup dry white wine
1 teaspoon salt
¼ teaspoon pepper

Cut away underside membrane of rock lobster tails using kitchen scissors. Pull meat out of shell and cut into ½-inch crosswise slices. Heat olive oil and sauté garlic, scallions, parsley and rock lobster slices. Sauté only until rock lobster meat loses its translucency and becomes opaque. Blend remaining ingredients, beat until smooth and stir into rock lobster mixture. Simmer together gently, stirring constantly, until flour is cooked and flavors are blended. The sauce will have a slightly curdled appearance like Chinese lobster sauce. Put into casserole and freeze. For service, thaw, and reheat in oven until mixture bubbles. Serve with steamed white rice.   *Yield: 8 servings*

Favorite recipe from **South African Rock Lobster Service Corp.**

BOOTH

Parmesan Crumb Fillet

1 pound **BOOTH Fish Fillets** (whiting, ocean catfish, turbot)
¼ cup melted butter or margarine
1 teaspoon lemon juice
1 teaspoon Worcestershire sauce
2 teaspoons instant minced onion
1 tablespoon dry bread crumbs
1 tablespoon grated Parmesan cheese

Defrost fillets. Place in a single layer in a greased baking dish. Combine butter, lemon juice, Worcestershire sauce, onion, bread crumbs and cheese. Blend well and spread over fish. Bake in preheated 350°F oven for 20-25 minutes, until fish flakes easily with a fork.

Lipton.

Scallops Elegante

⅓ cup **LIPTON®** Onion Butter*
½ pound mushrooms, sliced
1 pound scallops
½ cup dry white wine
1 tablespoon chopped parsley
2 tablespoons grated Parmesan cheese

In medium skillet, melt **LIPTON®** Onion Butter and cook mushrooms until golden. Add scallops, wine and parsley; simmer 5 minutes or until scallops are tender.

Turn mixture into 4 individual serving dishes or 1-quart baking dish; sprinkle with cheese and broil until golden brown. Serve, if desired, with toast points. *Makes 4 servings*

*Lipton® Onion Butter

Thoroughly blend 1 envelope **LIPTON® Onion Soup Mix** with ½ pound butter or margarine. Makes 1¼ cups. Refrigerate unused portion. Use on baked potatoes, as a sandwich spread or on cooked vegetables.

Shrimp Pernod®

24-30 shrimp (according to size)
2 oz. butter
1 small, finely chopped onion
2 lb. tomatoes skinned and chopped
1 pinch sugar
1 clove garlic
½ teaspoon chopped parsley
Salt and pepper
1 tablespoon **PERNOD®**, diluted with 1 tablespoon water
A little tomato paste

Poach the shrimp in salted water for 3-5 minutes (allow 5 minutes more if they are not shelled. Shell after they are poached.) Drain. Melt the butter in a large saucepan, then fry the onion slowly, without browning, for about 3 minutes. Add the tomatoes and other ingredients except the tomato paste and leave to simmer for about 30 minutes, stirring from time to time. Check the seasoning, and add tomato paste according to taste. Reheat the shrimp in the sauce and serve with rice. *Serves 4*

Shrimp Scampi with Zucchini

½ cup **LAND O LAKES®** Sweet Cream Butter
¼ cup chopped fresh parsley
2 Tbsp. chopped onion
1½ tsp. garlic salt
½ tsp. dill weed
1 Tbsp. lemon juice
24 fresh, med. size (3-inch) green shrimp, shelled, deveined, rinsed
2 cups (2 med.) sliced (¼-inch) zucchini
Cooked, hot rice

In heavy 10-inch skillet melt butter over med. heat (3 to 6 min.). Add remaining ingredients *except* rice; stir to blend. Cook over med. heat, stirring occasionally, until shrimp and zucchini are tender (5 to 7 min.). To serve, spoon 6 shrimp with zucchini and butter sauce over cooked rice. *Yield: 4 servings*

Sicilian Shrimp Parmigiana

Spread 6 ounces thawed **BRILLIANT Cooked Shrimp** in a single layer in a greased baking pan. Sprinkle with ½ teaspoon oregano and spoon 1 cup prepared marinara sauce evenly over shrimp and cover with ½ cup shredded mozzarella cheese. Broil until cheese melts and begins to brown. Serve over cooked macaroni.
Serves 3-4

Tuna and Green Beans, Italiano

2 (6½ oz.) cans tuna, drained
2 (16 oz.) cans Italian green beans, drained
1 (8½ oz.) can water chestnuts, drained and sliced
1 (10¾ oz.) can condensed cream of mushroom soup
1 cup plain yogurt
¼ cup finely chopped onions
¼ tsp. garlic powder
2 Tbsp. butter or margarine
2 cups (3-4 slices) soft **ROMAN MEAL®** Bread crumbs

Flake tuna into medium-size mixing bowl. Combine beans and water chestnuts with tuna. Blend together soup, yogurt, onions and garlic powder. Add to tuna mixture; toss lightly to distribute evenly. Spread in shallow 2-quart casserole dish. Melt butter in small pan over medium heat; add bread crumbs and brown lightly. Sprinkle crumbs over top of tuna mixture. Bake at 350°F for about 30 minutes. *Makes 8 servings, ¾ cup each*

Note: Serve this easy and nutritious main dish with buttered egg noodles and sliced tomatoes.

Baked Clams Italiano

1 (10½ ounce) can minced clams
2 tablespoons olive oil
1 tablespoon grated onion
1 tablespoon minced parsley
⅛ teaspoon oregano
¼ cup plus 2 tablespoons crumbled **HI HO CRACKERS®**
1 teaspoon garlic salt
2 tablespoons grated Parmesan cheese

Drain clams and reserve 3 tablespoons broth. Heat olive oil in small frying pan. Sauté onion, parsley, oregano and ¼ cup crumbled crackers for 2 minutes, or until onion is golden. Remove from heat and mix with clams, 3 tablespoons broth, and garlic salt. Spoon into a dozen clam or aluminum shells. Sprinkle lightly with a mixture made of 2 tablespoons Parmesan cheese and 2 tablespoons cracker crumbs. On baking sheet, bake in 375°F. oven for 25 minutes, or until crusty on top. *Yield: 6 servings*

Eggs & Cheese

The incredible edible egg™

Pizza Frittata

¼ cup chopped onion
¼ cup chopped green pepper
2 tablespoons butter
8 eggs
¼ cup water
2 ounces sliced pepperoni (about ½ cup)
1 medium tomato, chopped
½ teaspoon Italian herb seasoning
¼ teaspoon salt
½ cup (2 oz.) shredded mozzarella cheese

In 10-inch ovenproof* omelet or fry pan cook onion and green pepper in butter until tender but not browned.

Beat together eggs and all remaining ingredients except cheese. Pour egg mixture over onion-green pepper mixture in omelet pan. Cook without stirring over low to medium heat until eggs are set at edges but still runny in center, 7 to 9 minutes.

Sprinkle with cheese. Broil 5 to 6 inches from heat until cheese melts and browns lightly, about 3 minutes. Cut in wedges to serve.

4 to 6 servings

*To make handle ovenproof, cover completely with aluminum foil.
Favorite recipe from the **American Egg Board**

Long Grain and Wild Rice Frittata

6 slices bacon
2⅓ cups water
1 package (6 ounces) UNCLE BEN'S® Original Long Grain & Wild Rice
1 medium zucchini, chopped (about 1 cup)
1 teaspoon salt
1 medium tomato, chopped
8 eggs
¾ cup dairy sour cream
½ cup grated Parmesan cheese

Fry bacon in 10-inch ovenproof skillet*; remove and reserve. Drain all but 2 tablespoons drippings. Add water, and contents of rice and seasoning packets to skillet. Bring to a boil. Cover tightly and cook over low heat until all water is absorbed, about 25 minutes. While rice is cooking, sprinkle zucchini with salt; let stand at least 10 minutes. Press out excess moisture. Stir zucchini and tomato into rice in skillet; press into even layer. Beat eggs with sour cream; pour over rice mixture. Crumble reserved bacon; sprinkle bacon and cheese over egg mixture. Bake at 375° F. 25 to 30 minutes or until firm and puffy. Let stand 5 minutes; cut into wedges.

Makes 6 servings

*If ovenproof skillet is not available, prepare rice and vegetable mixture in skillet; spoon into well-greased deep 10-inch pie dish. Pour egg mixture over rice; sprinkle with bacon and cheese and bake at 350° F. until firm and puffy, about 30 minutes.

Broccoli Frittata

2½ tablespoons finely chopped onion
2 teaspoons butter or margarine
1 package (10 ounces) frozen chopped broccoli, cooked and drained
½ small clove garlic, crushed (optional)
1 cup cooked DORE® Rice
2½ tablespoons grated Parmesan cheese
2 eggs, slightly beaten
¼ cup milk
½ teaspoon salt
Dash of ground black pepper
⅓ cup grated mozzarella cheese

Sauté onion in butter until tender but not brown. Add broccoli, garlic, rice, and Parmesan cheese; mix well. Combine eggs, milk, and seasonings. Stir into rice mixture. Turn into a well-buttered shallow 1-quart casserole. Top with mozzarella cheese. Bake at 350° for 20 to 25 minutes or until set. *Makes 2 servings*

Frittata

1 jar (6 oz.) marinated artichoke hearts, chopped
2 tablespoons butter
2 cups sliced DOLE® Fresh Mushrooms
¼ cup chopped green onion
6 eggs
½ teaspoon garlic salt
2 tablespoons white wine
2 tablespoons grated Parmesan cheese

Drain artichoke marinade into a 10-inch oven-proof skillet. Add butter and melt. Sauté mushrooms until golden. Add artichoke hearts and green onion tossing until heated through. Turn heat to medium. Beat eggs with garlic salt and wine until blended. Pour over mushroom mixture. *DO NOT STIR.* Cook slowly until sides are bubbly. Sprinkle with cheese and place under broiler until cheese is browned and eggs are set. Serve directly from skillet.

Makes 4 servings

Crab Frittata Florentine

1 (6 oz.) can PACIFIC PEARL Snow Crab
⅓ cup chopped onion
3 Tbsp. butter or margarine
6 large eggs, beaten
2 Tbsp. cream
½ cup chopped, cooked spinach
¼ tsp. salt
Dash hot pepper sauce
¼ cup grated Parmesan cheese

Drain crab meat. Flake and cut large pieces into chunks. Sauté onion in butter or margarine until tender. Mix together eggs, cream, spinach, salt, hot pepper sauce and crab meat. Pour over onion in skillet and cook slowly over low heat until set. Sprinkle cheese on top and place under broiler, about 4 inches from heat, until lightly browned. Let frittata stand for a minute or two, then cut in wedges and serve. *Makes approximately 4 servings*

TABASCO®

Skillet Eggs Florentine

¼ cup butter or margarine
1 large onion, thinly sliced (1 cup)
2 tablespoons flour
2 cups milk
½ teaspoon **TABASCO® Pepper Sauce**
¼ teaspoon salt
Pinch nutmeg
1 can (4 ounces) sliced mushrooms, drained
1 package (10 ounces) frozen chopped spinach,
    thawed, drained
8 eggs

In large skillet melt butter; sauté onions until golden. Stir in flour; cook 1 minute. Gradually add milk; stir until mixture boils and thickens. Stir in **TABASCO® Sauce**, salt and nutmeg. Add mushrooms and spinach. With back of a spoon make 8 indentations in spinach mixture. Break one egg into each well. Cover. Cook about 5 minutes until egg whites are set. *Yield: 4 servings*

Contadina

Eggplant Parmesan

1¾ pounds eggplant
⅓ cup oil
2 cups (1 pound) ricotta cheese
1⅓ cups (12-ounce can) **CONTADINA® Italian Paste**
1⅓ cups (1 can) water
½ cup fine dry bread crumbs
2 tablespoons Parmesan cheese

Peel eggplant; slice into ¼-inch slices. Fry on both sides, in oil, in large skillet until tender. (Add more oil if necessary.) Drain on paper towels. Place half of eggplant slices on bottom of 12 x 7½ x 2-inch baking dish. Spread half of ricotta cheese over eggplant. Combine Italian Paste and water; mix thoroughly. Pour half of mixture over ricotta. Combine bread crumbs and Parmesan cheese. Sprinkle half over top of Italian Paste mixture. Repeat layers. Bake in moderate oven (350° F.) 30 minutes or until sauce is bubbly. Cut in squares to serve. *Makes 6 servings*

Sargento Eggplant Parmesan

2 medium eggplant, peeled, cut into ½ inch slices
Salt
Flour for coating
Olive oil for frying
2 cups tomato sauce
8 oz. **SARGENTO Shredded Mozzarella Cheese**
½ cup **SARGENTO Grated Parmesan and Romano Blend Cheese**
3 Tbsp. butter

Cut eggplant into ½ inch slices. Sprinkle both sides lightly with salt and place between paper towel. Place a wooden board or heavy weight on top of eggplant and let stand at least 30 minutes. Rinse and pat dry with paper towels. Dip in flour and fry slices in olive oil until lightly brown.

Place a single layer of eggplant in a buttered dish. Cover with ⅓ of tomato sauce and also ⅓ of shredded Mozzarella and ⅓ of Parmesan and Romano cheese. Continue to layer eggplant, sauce, and cheeses for two more layers; end with Parmesan and Romano cheese. Dot with butter and bake at 400° degrees for 30 minutes.
Makes 4 servings

Vegetables

Beans Italiano

1 lb. dry navy beans
6 cups water
2 medium onions, grated
1 clove garlic, mashed
1 bay leaf
2 tablespoons fresh chopped parsley
½ teaspoon dill seed
Salt and pepper to taste
½ cup olive or vegetable oil
2 cups canned tomatoes, drained
3 small sweet pickles, chopped
½ cup green stuffed olives, chopped
1 cup celery, chopped
Grated cheese

Wash and sort beans. Combine beans and water in large saucepan. Bring to a boil and cook 2 minutes. Remove from heat, cover and let stand one hour. Add onion, garlic and seasonings; simmer about 2 hours until beans are tender, adding water if needed. Separately cook tomato, pickles, olives and celery in oil until tender. Mix vegetables and beans and pour mixture into 2½ quart casserole. Cover and bake at 275°F. about 2 hours. Uncover and sprinkle with grated cheese. Continue baking until cheese is browned. *Makes 10-12 servings*

Favorite recipe from **Michigan Bean Commission**

Green Beans Italian

3 Tbsp. **LAND O LAKES® Sweet Cream Butter**
½ cup (½ med.) onion, cut into ¼ inch rings
9-oz. pkg. frozen cut green beans, thawed, drained
2 Tbsp. sliced (⅛ inch) ripe olives
1 tsp. basil leaves
½ tsp. salt
⅛ tsp. garlic powder
½ cup (½ med.) cubed (½ inch) tomato

In 2-qt. saucepan melt butter. Stir in onion. Cook, uncovered, over med. heat, stirring occasionally, until crisply tender (3 to 5 min.). Stir in remaining ingredients *except* tomato. Cover; continue cooking, stirring occasionally, until vegetables are crisply tender (5 to 7 min.). Stir in tomato. Cover; continue cooking 1 min.
Yield: 5 (½ cup) servings
(Continued)

MICROWAVE METHOD:
In 1½-qt. casserole melt butter on high (40 to 50 sec.). Stir in onion. Cover; cook on high 2½ min. Stir in remaining ingredients *except* tomato. Cover; cook on high, stirring after ½ the time until vegetables are crisply tender (3 to 4 min.). Stir in tomato. Cover; cook on high 1 min. Let stand 1 min.

THE ORIGINAL WORCESTERSHIRE

Green Beans, Italian-Style

1 package (9 oz.) frozen cut green beans, slightly thawed
1 can (1 lb.) stewed tomatoes
1 teaspoon cornstarch
1 teaspoon **LEA & PERRINS Worcestershire Sauce**
½ teaspoon basil leaves

In a small saucepan combine all ingredients. Bring to boiling point. Reduce heat; simmer until beans are tender.

Yield: 6 portions

Brown's Best Italian Casserole

1 lb. **BROWN'S BEST Great Northern Beans,** prepare Basic Recipe*
1 cup olive oil
2 cups onions–coarsely chopped
4 cloves garlic–chop fine
2 cups celery–coarsely chopped
4 tablespoons fresh parsley–snipped
1 teaspoon dried crushed thyme
½ teaspoon dried crushed sweet basil
½ teaspoon black pepper
2 cups canned tomatoes
½ cup bean liquid
½ cup tomato juice
Grated Parmesan cheese

After beans are tender, drain and reserve liquid. Heat oil over low heat, add onion, garlic, celery. Sauté until tender. Add all remaining ingredients except cheese, and bring to a boil. Add to beans and mix lightly with a wooden spoon. Turn into a 3 quart casserole. Cover and bake in 350 oven 1 hour. Remove from oven, sprinkle generously with Parmesan cheese. Return to oven, uncovered, until cheese is melted—about 10-12 minutes. Serve hot with additional cheese to sprinkle on each serving.

*Basic Recipe

1 pound **BROWN'S BEST Great Northerns, Pintos, Red Beans, Large Limas** or **Baby Limas**
12 cups water
2 teaspoons salt

Wash beans thoroughly, removing any off colored beans. Use a large heavy pot—approximately 3 times the amount of the water and beans. Bring the salted water and beans to a boiling point. Boil

2 minutes only. Cover. Remove from heat. Allow to stand 1 hour. Return to the heat and bring to a boil. Reduce the heat and simmer slowly until tender. We suggest always cooking at least 1 lb. of **BROWN'S BEST** beans at a time. If the recipe calls for less, the remainder can always be frozen to use at a later date.

Italian-Style Green Beans

1 Golden Delicious apple, coarsely chopped
1 can (8 oz.) whole tomatoes, chopped, undrained
1 can (8 oz.) cut green beans, drained
2 tablespoons chopped green pepper
2 tablespoons chopped onion
¼ teaspoon salt
Dash pepper

Combine all ingredients; cover and simmer 5 minutes. Serve in sauce dishes with broiled chicken.

Makes four 56-calorie servings

Favorite recipe from **The Apple Growers of Washington State**

Featherweight®

Herbed Green Beans

(Sodium Reduced)

1 can (15½ oz.) **FEATHERWEIGHT® Green Beans,** drained
2 Tbsp. unsalted butter
½ cup onion, chopped
¼ cup celery, chopped
1 clove garlic, minced
¼ tsp. rosemary
¼ tsp. basil
¼ tsp. **FEATHERWEIGHT® K-Salt**

Melt butter, add all ingredients and cook for 10 minutes. Add beans, toss and heat through. *Serves 6-7*

Note: Calories reduced if butter is eliminated.

Bertolli® Stuffed Artichokes

4 medium artichokes
Juice of 1 lemon
1 rib celery, thinly sliced
½ red pepper, cut into strips
¼ cup finely chopped onion
1 tablespoon **BERTOLLI® Olive Oil**
1 cup cooked peas
2 tablespoons walnut pieces
¼ cup **BERTOLLI® Olive Oil**
1 tablespoon **BERTOLLI® Red Wine Vinegar**
1 teaspoon sugar
Dash each salt and pepper

Cut stem and 1-inch top from artichokes; cut tips off leaves. Rub artichokes with lemon juice; heat to boiling in 2-inches water in saucepan. Reduce heat; simmer covered until tender, about 30 minutes. Drain; cool. Separate top leaves; remove chokes with spoon.

Sauté celery, pepper and onion in 1 tablespoon oil in skillet 4 minutes. Stir in peas and walnuts. Mix remaining ingredients; stir into vegetables. Spoon vegetables into center of artichokes. Serve hot or refrigerate and serve cold. *Makes 4 servings*

Italian Eggplant

12 double **SUNSHINE® KRISPY® Crackers**
2 tablespoons grated Parmesan cheese
1 egg
1 tablespoon water
Salt to taste
½ teaspoon pepper
1 medium eggplant (about 1¼ pounds)
Buttery flavored vegetable oil for frying

With rolling pin, crush crackers into very fine crumbs between waxed paper. There should be about 1 cup. Stir with the cheese and put in a shallow plate. Beat egg well with water, salt and pepper in another shallow plate. Cut unpeeled eggplant into slices about ¼ inch thick. Dip slices into egg mixture, drain a bit and coat well with crumb mixture. Let sit on waxed paper for about 15 minutes to set the crumbs. Put about ¼ inch oil in large skillet and place over moderate heat. Cook the slices on both sides until golden brown. Add more oil as necessary. Drain on paper towels in warm place. *Yield: 4 to 6 servings*

Cheesy-Roman Tomatoes

5 large tomatoes
¼ cup soft bread crumbs
¼ cup shredded **PIZZA-MATE®**
1 Tbsp. butter or margarine—melted
Snipped parsley
Salt & pepper

Slice off tops of tomatoes. Cut zigzag edges; season with salt and pepper. Combine crumbs, **PIZZA-MATE®** and butter; sprinkle over tomatoes. Garnish with parsley. Heat tomatoes on foil over hot coals, or bake at 375° til warmed through. Serve immediately. *Makes 5 servings*

Spinach Italienne

2 packages frozen chopped spinach
1½ cups crushed **KEEBLER® HARVEST WHEAT® Crackers**
3 eggs, beaten
1½ cups ricotta cheese
4 tablespoons butter
¾ cup milk
¼ teaspoon nutmeg or paprika
¼ teaspoon salt
½ cup grated Parmesan cheese
Dash of white pepper

Cook spinach according to package directions; drain thoroughly and while still hot, add ricotta cheese and stir over low heat until well blended. Add all other ingredients except **HARVEST WHEAT®** cracker crumbs and Parmesan.

Place half of spinach mixture in a square pan which has been greased. Top with half of the **HARVEST WHEAT®** cracker crumbs. Pour rest of spinach mixture over first layer. Top with cheese and remainder of crumbs. *(Continued)*

Bake in 350° oven for 30 minutes until puffed and golden. Makes 6 large servings; use as a main dish or delicious vegetable combination. It also reheats well.

Pizza Style Tater Tots®

4 cups frozen **ORE-IDA® TATER TOTS®***
¼ tsp. salt
1 cup grated Cheddar cheese
⅓ cup **HEINZ Tomato Ketchup**
¼ tsp. Italian herb seasoning

1. Place frozen **TATER TOTS®** close together on lightly greased baking sheet and bake in oven at 450° F for 12-15 minutes until desired brownness. Remove from oven and sprinkle with salt and grated cheese.
2. Combine ketchup and Italian herbs; drizzle over **TATER TOTS®**. Bake another 5 minutes. *Yield: 4-6 servings*

*May also be used with the following **ORE-IDA®** products:
TATER TOTS® with Bacon
TATER TOTS® with Onion

Vegetables Italiano

Chop:
　　2 Tbsp. green onion
Drain, reserving liquid:
　　1 can (16 oz.) **DEL MONTE Cut Green Beans**
Sauté onion in:
　　1 Tbsp. butter or margarine
Add:
　　1 can (8 oz.) **DEL MONTE Stewed Tomatoes**
　　⅛ tsp. thyme
　　Dash pepper
Dissolve in reserved liquid:
　　1½ tsp. cornstarch

Add to tomato-onion mixture. Cook over low heat, stirring constantly, until thickened. Add beans; heat.

Stuffed Green Peppers Provencale

4 large green peppers
1 onion, chopped
½ pound Italian sausage meat
1 tablespoon **POLLY-O® Butter**
2 tablespoons tomato paste dissolved in 3 cups warm broth or bouillon
1 cup rice, uncooked
3 tablespoons **POLLY-O® Grated Parmesan or Romano Cheese**
6 ounces **POLLY-O® Mozzarella**, grated

Preheat oven to 350°. Cut a slice from stem end of peppers, remove seeds and parboil 5 minutes. Crumble sausage into a large skillet and brown with onion in butter until onion is soft and transparent. Add rice and stir until rice is lightly browned. Add dissolved tomato paste and salt to taste. Cover and simmer until rice is barely tender and has absorbed liquid. Add grated cheese and blend. Stuff peppers with rice mixture, piling stuffing high. Top generously with mozzarella, and dot with butter. Arrange peppers in well-greased baking dish and bake uncovered about 30 minutes, or until mozzarella melts and is golden brown.

4 servings

Stir Glazed Zucchini

2 small unpared zucchini
1 tsp. diet margarine
¼ tsp. garlic powder
Black pepper
1 envelope ESTEE® Low Sodium Instant Cream of
   Tomato Soup Mix
½ cup water
⅛ tsp. oregano
⅛ tsp. basil
½ tsp. dehydrated minced onion

Cut unpared zucchini into ½ inch thick slices, then sauté over medium-high heat in diet margarine and 1 tsp. water. Season with garlic powder and a dash of black pepper. Reduce heat to low and simmer, covered, for 2-3 minutes. In small bowl, mix 1 envelope ESTEE® Low Sodium Instant Cream of Tomato Soup Mix into ½ cup boiling water and stir to blend. Add oregano, basil, and dehydrated minced onion. Pour tomato soup mixture over zucchini, toss gently, and serve. Season to taste with ESTEE® Salt-Free Vegetable Seasoning.

Makes 2 servings, ½ cup per serving

NUTRITION INFORMATION

CAL	CHO	PRO	FAT	CHOL	NA
55	9g	3g	1g		50mg

Zucchini-Stuffed Tomatoes

1 cup (4-ounces) P & R Rings, uncooked
6 to 8 medium tomatoes
½ cup grated zucchini
1 cup cottage cheese
½ teaspoon basil
¼ teaspoon salt
⅛ teaspoon pepper

Cook Rings according to package directions; drain well. Cool. (Rinse with cold water to cool quickly; drain well.) Remove core from tomatoes; scoop pulp from tomatoes leaving a ½-inch shell. Combine ½ cup chopped tomato pulp, zucchini, cottage cheese, basil, salt and pepper in medium bowl; add cooled Rings and toss. Fill tomato shells; chill. Serve on lettuce leaves with wheat crackers, if desired.

6 to 8 servings

VARIATION:

Top tomatoes with shredded mozzarella cheese; place under broiler several minutes until cheese melts. Serve immediately.

Dorothy's Stir-Fry Zucchini with Parmesan Cheese

4-5 medium zucchini
⅛ tsp. oregano
⅛ tsp. basil
½ tsp. WITT'S Flavormost Seasoning
1 Tbsp. grated Parmesan cheese
⅛ tsp. coarse ground black pepper (optional)

Cut zucchini in strips, and sauté in frying pan or wok, adding oregano, basil, WITT'S Flavormost Seasoning, and pepper (if desired). Sauté until tender. Just before turning off heat, stir in Parmesan cheese. Serve hot.

Serves 4

Rice

Shrimp Risotto

1 (6 oz.) pkg. WAKEFIELD® Shrimp
1 small onion, sliced
1 cup sliced mushrooms
1 cup sliced celery
½ cup chopped green pepper
1 pkg. herb and butter rice mix
¼ cup melted butter
2 cups water
¼ cup white wine
¼ cup grated Parmesan cheese

Thaw and drain shrimp. Sauté vegetables and rice in butter. Add water and contents of seasoning packet from rice; heat to boil. Cover; simmer 15 minutes, stirring occasionally. Stir in remaining ingredients. Cover; simmer 5 minutes longer or until heated through.

Baked Rice with Cheese

1-6 oz. package SHOAL LAKE Pure Canadian Wild
   Rice
1 Tbsp. butter
½ onion chopped
¼ tsp. garlic powder
2 tsp. Worcestershire sauce
1 Tbsp. minced parsley
1½ cups chicken broth
⅔ cup dry wine
1 cup cubed sharp Cheddar cheese

Melt butter in a skillet; add onions and cook until tender. Stir in the wild rice and continue cooking until rice is golden. Add garlic powder, Worcestershire sauce, parsley, chicken broth and wine. Heat to boiling. Stir in the cheese. Turn into a buttered 1½ quart casserole and bake in a 350° oven for 2 hours. Serve hot as a meat accompaniment.

Serves 6

White Risotto with Mushrooms

½ pound fresh mushrooms, sliced
1 garlic clove
1 tablespoon olive or vegetable oil
2 tablespoons butter or margarine
1 cup thinly sliced onion
1 cup **UNCLE BEN'S® CONVERTED® Brand Rice**
2¼ cups chicken broth
¼ cup dry white wine
1½ teaspoons salt
¼ teaspoon white pepper
¼ cup freshly grated Parmesan cheese
2 tablespoons chopped parsley

Sauté mushrooms and garlic in olive oil in 10-inch skillet until mushrooms are tender, but not brown. Remove and reserve mushrooms; discard garlic. Add butter to skillet. Sauté onion until tender. Add rice; cook, stirring constantly, 5 minutes. Add chicken broth, mushrooms, wine, salt and pepper. Bring to boil; reduce heat. Cover tightly and simmer 20 minutes. Remove from heat. Stir in cheese and parsley. Let stand, covered, until all liquid is absorbed, about 5 minutes.   *Makes 6 servings*

Italian Rice & Cheese Bake

4 teaspoons **WYLER'S® Chicken-Flavor Instant Bouillon** or **4 Chicken-Flavor Bouillon Cubes**
2 cups boiling water
1 cup uncooked long grain rice
½ teaspoon dry mustard
¼ teaspoon pepper
¾ cup chopped green pepper
¾ cup chopped onion
2 tablespoons margarine or butter
2 cups (8 ounces) shredded mozzarella cheese
2 tablespoons chopped pimiento
2 cups milk
3 eggs
2 tablespoons grated Parmesan cheese

Preheat oven to 325°. In medium saucepan, dissolve bouillon in water. Stir in rice, mustard and pepper; bring to a boil. Reduce heat; cover and simmer 15 minutes or until rice is tender. Remove from heat. In small saucepan, cook green pepper and onion in margarine until tender. In greased 2½-quart shallow baking dish (12x7-inch), layer *half each* the rice, the onion mixture and the mozzarella cheese. Repeat layering; top with pimiento. Beat milk and eggs together; pour over rice. Sprinkle with Parmesan cheese. Bake uncovered 40 to 50 minutes. Let stand 10 minutes before serving. Cut into squares. Refrigerate leftovers.   *Makes 8 servings*

Italian Rice Casserole

2 bags **SUCCESS® Rice**
2 eggs, slightly beaten
½ cup grated Parmesan cheese (divided)
1 pound lean ground beef
2 jars (15½ oz. each) extra thick spaghetti sauce
2 cups mozzarella cheese, shredded
1 cup Swiss cheese, shredded
¼-½ cup cottage cheese, small curd
2 tablespoons grated Parmesan cheese

Cook rice according to package directions. Cool slightly. Add the eggs and ¼ cup Parmesan cheese, mix well.

Brown the ground beef, drain off the excess fat. Add the spaghetti sauce and continue cooking until thoroughly heated. Combine the cheeses, reserving 2 tablespoons Parmesan cheese, and mix well. Onto the bottom of a 13 x 9-inch glass dish or a 3 quart casserole, spoon half of the rice mixture. Cover with one half of the cheese mixture. Spoon one half of the meat mixture over the cheese. Repeat the layers. Sprinkle the top with 2 tablespoons of Parmesan cheese. Bake at 375° F. for 20-30 minutes, until thoroughly heated.

Desserts

Blueberry Zuppa Inglese

1 pkg. (14½ oz.) angel food cake mix
2 pkgs. (3¼ oz. ea.) vanilla pudding and pie filling
3 cups milk
Grated rind of 1 lemon
½ cup sherry
1 can (1 lb. 5 oz.) blueberry pie filling
1 can (15 oz.) blueberries, drained
Whipped cream or whipped topping

Prepare cake mix according to package directions and bake according to package directions in a 10 x 4-inch tube pan. Cool cake in pan. Combine pudding mix and milk and grated lemon rind. Cook while stirring until pudding bubbles and thickens. Cool. Remove cake from pan as directed on package and cut with a serrated knife with a sawing motion into three layers. Place one layer on serving platter and sprinkle with ⅓ of the sherry, spread with ⅓ of the blueberry pie filling, sprinkle with ⅓ of the blueberries and spread with ⅓ of the pudding. Repeat using other two layers. On third layer, reserve a few blueberries. Decorate top with whipped cream or topping and reserved blueberries. Chill until ready to serve.

Favorite recipe from **North American Blueberry Council**

Tia Maria
Chocolate Cake Florence

500 mL or 2 cups sifted cake flour
10 mL or 2 teaspoons baking powder
1 dash salt
125 mL or ½ cup butter
500 mL or 2 cups sugar
4 eggs, separated
4 squares unsweetened chocolate, melted
5 mL or 1 teaspoon vanilla
325 mL or 1⅓ cups milk
60 mL or ¼ cup **TIA MARIA®**
Chopped nuts

Sift flour with baking powder and salt. Cream butter; add 375 mL or 1½ cups of the sugar gradually and blend until light and fluffy. Beat in egg yolks. Add chocolate and vanilla. Add flour alternately with milk, mixing well after each addition. Beat egg whites until stiff but not dry; add remaining sugar and fold into batter. Turn into two 9-inch layer pans which have been buttered and floured. Bake in moderate oven 350°F (180°C) 35 minutes. Cool. Pour 30 mL or 2 tablespoons **TIA MARIA®** over each layer and frost with Florence Icing.* Dust sides with chopped nuts.

*Florence Icing

Melt 60 mL or 4 tablespoons butter in a saucepan; add 500 mL or 2 cups sugar and 125 mL or ½ cup milk. Bring to a boil stirring constantly then cook over low heat 10 minutes or until temperature reaches 236°F or 115°C. Melt 2 squares unsweetened chocolate; add 125 mL or ½ cup **TIA MARIA®**. Stir into butter mixture. Remove from heat and beat icing until thick enough to spread. If icing hardens before cake is frosted, soften with a little hot water.

Saronno Zuccotto

1 10¾ ounce frozen pound cake, thawed
⅓ cup **AMARETTO DI SARONNO®**
2 cups (1 pint) heavy cream whipped
½ cup toasted sliced almonds
½ cup chopped pecans
½ cup halved candied cherries
1 cup mini-chocolate chips
Additional whipped cream, candied cherries, almonds and pecans

Cut pound cake into slices, slightly less than ½ inch thick. Cut each slice of cake diagonally into two triangles. Line a 1½-quart round-bottomed bowl with damp cheesecloth. Place triangles in the same direction so that the crust on the cake will make a swirled design. Sprinkle cake with **AMARETTO DI SARONNO®**. Whip cream until very stiff. Fold almonds, pecans, cherries and half of the mini-chips into half of the cream. Spread the cream evenly in the cake-lined bowl, covering the cake and making a hollow in the center. Chill. Melt remaining mini-chips, cool and fold into remaining cream. Spoon chocolate cream into hollow. Cover with remaining cake slices. Chill overnight. Use cheesecloth to pull zuccotto out of bowl. Place on cake plate and decorate with rosettes of whipped cream topped with cherries, sliced almonds and pecans.

Makes 6 to 8 servings

Chocolate Ricotta Cassata

1 pound cake (9 inches by 5 inches)
1½ cups (15 ounces) ricotta cheese
2 tablespoons whipping cream
¼ cup sugar
3 tablespoons orange-flavored liqueur or orange juice concentrate, undiluted
1 tablespoon each: coarsely chopped red candied cherries, green candied cherries, candied pineapple
½ cup **HERSHEY'S®** Semi-Sweet Mini Chips

Cut the cake horizontally into 4 slices about ½-inch thick. Press ricotta cheese through a coarse sieve into a bowl (or cream in blender). Add cream, sugar and orange-flavored liqueur or orange juice concentrate. Beat until smooth. Fold in candied fruits and **Mini Chips**. Place bottom slice of cake on a serving plate. Spread cheese filling generously between cake layers. Gently press loaf together. Chill; meanwhile prepare Satin Frosting*. Frost and "ripen" 24 hours.

Serves 10 to 12
(Continued)

*Satin Frosting

1 cup (5.75-ounce package) **HERSHEY'S®** Milk Chocolate Chips
½ cup **HERSHEY'S®** Semi-Sweet Mini Chips
3 tablespoons butter
¼ cup milk
3 tablespoons light corn syrup
½ teaspoon instant coffee (optional)
2 cups confectioners' sugar

Combine milk chocolate chips, **Mini Chips,** butter, milk, corn syrup and instant coffee in small saucepan. Place over low heat, stirring occasionally, until chips are melted. Pour into small mixer bowl. Add confectioners' sugar; beat until smooth. Chill 15 to 20 minutes or until of spreading consistency.

Spread frosting evenly over top, sides and ends of Cassata. To decorate, pipe remaining frosting through decorator tube. Cover loosely with aluminum foil and let Cassata "ripen" in refrigerator at least 24 hours before serving. *About 2 cups frosting*

Note: Also can be used to fill and frost an 8- or 9-inch layer cake.

Cheese-Filled Coffee Cake Wreath

1 frozen **SARA LEE** Butter Streusel Coffee Cake
½ cup ricotta cheese *OR* cottage cheese
1 tablespoon grated lemon peel
½ teaspoon lemon juice
2 tablespoons chopped candied cherries
3 red candied cherries, halved
3 green candied cherries, halved
About 2 tablespoons sliced almonds

Cut frozen Coffee Cake lengthwise into 2 layers. Beat together ricotta cheese, lemon peel and juice; spread on bottom layer. Sprinkle on chopped cherries. Replace cake top; cut into 6 pieces. Arrange cherry halves and almonds on cake top to resemble a wreath. Heat in preheated 350° F. oven 15 minutes.

Makes 6 servings

Tantalizing Tortoni

2 cups crushed **SUNSHINE®** Vanilla Wafers (60 wafers)
2 cups heavy cream
½ cup chopped toasted almonds
¼ cup chopped candied cherries
¼ cup confectioners' sugar
1 teaspoon rum extract

Combine 1½ cups crushed **SUNSHINE®** Vanilla Wafers with 1 cup heavy cream, almonds, cherries, confectioners' sugar, and rum extract. Let stand for 15 minutes. Whip remaining 1 cup heavy cream until stiff. Fold into cookie mixture. Spoon into individual serving dishes. Sprinkle top of each dessert with the remaining **Vanilla Wafer** crumbs. Freeze at least 2 hours or overnight.

Yield: 6-8 servings

Pineapple Tortoni Sicilian

1 can (20 oz.) **DOLE®** **Crushed Pineapple in Juice**
1 large, ripe **DOLE®** **Banana**, peeled
1 pkg. (3-¾ oz.) instant vanilla pudding and pie filling mix
½ cup dairy sour cream
½ cup chopped maraschino cherries
½ cup toasted flaked coconut
½ cup chopped walnuts
1 cup whipping cream, whipped
Fresh mint

Drain pineapple well, reserving 1 cup juice. Slice banana into blender; whir until pureed. Combine pudding mix, reserved juice and sour cream. Beat until smooth. Stir in pureed banana, pineapple, cherries, coconut and walnuts. Fold in whipped cream. Spoon into 6 (1-cup) dessert dishes. Freeze overnight. Let tortoni stand at room temperature 20 to 30 minutes to thaw slightly before serving. Garnish with mint. *Makes 6 servings*

Chocolate Biscuit Tortoni

⅓ cup **HERSHEY'S®** **Cocoa**
½ cup sugar
1½ cups heavy cream
1 cup almond macaroon or vanilla wafer crumbs (about 24 cookies)
½ cup chopped toasted almonds
¼ cup maraschino cherries, drained and chopped
1 to 2 tablespoons rum or dry sherry
1 teaspoon vanilla

Combine cocoa and sugar in mixer bowl; add heavy cream. Beat on low speed to blend; beat on medium speed until stiff. Reserve ¼ cup macaroon crumbs; fold remaining ingredients into chocolate whipped cream. Divide among 12 small dessert dishes or paper-lined medium muffin cups 2¼ x 1¼ inches. Sprinkle with reserved crumbs and decorate with a maraschino cherry half. Freeze until firm, about 4 hours. *12 servings*

EAGLE®BRAND

Tortoni Mold

1 (14-ounce) can **EAGLE®** **Brand Sweetened Condensed Milk** (NOT evaporated milk)
3 egg yolks, beaten*
¼ cup light rum
2 teaspoons vanilla extract
⅔ cup coconut macaroon crumbs (about 5 large cookies)
½ to ¾ cup toasted slivered almonds
⅓ cup chopped maraschino cherries
2 cups (1 pint) **BORDEN®** **Whipping Cream,** whipped
Additional maraschino cherries, toasted slivered almonds and mint leaves for garnish, optional

In large bowl, combine all ingredients except whipped cream and garnish; mix well. Fold in whipped cream. Pour into lightly oiled 1½-quart mold; cover with aluminum foil. Freeze 6 hours or until firm. Using a hot cloth on outside of mold, unmold onto serving plate. Garnish with cherries, almonds and mint leaves if desired. Return leftovers to freezer. *Makes 12 to 15 servings*

*Use only Grade A clean, uncracked eggs.

Dubonnet Tortoni

¾ cup sugar
¼ cup water
5 egg yolks, beaten
⅜ cup **DUBONNET** **Rouge Aperitif Wine**
2 cups heavy cream, whipped

In saucepan combine sugar and water. Bring to a boil and boil for 5 minutes. Stir into egg yolks and stir over hot, but not boiling water, until custard is thick. Stir in **DUBONNET** **Rouge** and fold in heavy cream. Freeze in home freezer. *Makes 5 cups*

AMARETTO di SARONNO®

Saronno Panettone

1 package (13¾ ounces) hot roll mix, yeast included
½ cup lukewarm **AMARETTO DI SARONNO®**
Grated rind of 1 lemon
6 eggs
⅓ cup sugar
½ cup soft butter or margarine
½ cup raisins or currants
½ cup chopped candied orange peel
1½ cups sifted confectioners' sugar
2 tablespoons **AMARETTO DI SARONNO®**

Remove yeast from mix and pour into a large bowl. Stir in **AMARETTO DI SARONNO®**. Let stand until yeast is dissolved. Add lemon rind, eggs, sugar and butter or margarine and beat with an electric mixer until smooth. Add flour from hot roll mix and beat until dough is smooth and velvety. Fold in raisins or currants and orange peel. Pour dough into a greased and floured 2-pound coffee can. Let dough rise in a warm place, covered lightly with a piece of wax paper, until it comes to the top of the can. Bake in a preheated moderate oven (350°) for 40 to 45 minutes, or until cake sounds hollow when thumped. Let cool in can for 10 minutes, then unmold. Cool. Mix confectioners' sugar with **AMARETTO DI SARONNO®** and spoon over panettone. Cut into wedges to serve. *Makes 1 panettone*

Panettone
(Pah-neh-toh-nee)

4¼ to 4¾ cups all-purpose flour
2 packages **RED STAR®** **Instant Blend Dry Yeast**
½ cup sugar
1½ teaspoons anise seeds
1 teaspoon salt
½ cup milk
½ cup water
¼ cup butter or margarine
¾ teaspoon vanilla
2 eggs
½ cup raisins
½ cup chopped nuts
⅓ cup chopped candied fruit
1 egg, slightly beaten
1 tablespoon water

In large mixer bowl, combine 1¾ cups flour, yeast, sugar, anise seeds and salt; mix well. In saucepan, heat milk, water and butter until warm (120-130°; butter does not need to melt). Add to flour mixture. Add vanilla and eggs. Blend at low speed until moistened; beat 3 minutes at medium speed. By hand, gradually stir in raisins, nuts, candied fruit and enough remaining flour to make a soft dough. Knead on floured surface, 5 to 8 minutes. Place in greased bowl, turning to grease top. Cover; let rise in warm place until double, about 1 hour.

Punch down dough. Divide into 2 parts. On lightly floured surface, shape each half into a round loaf. Place on greased large cookie sheet. Cover; let rise in warm place until double, 30 to 45 minutes. Combine egg and water; brush loaves. Bake at 375° for 30 to 35 minutes until golden brown. Remove from cookie sheet; cool.   *2 round loaves*

Italian Panettone

    2 packages active dry yeast
    ½ cup sugar
    2 teaspoons salt
    6 to 6½ cups flour
    1 cup water
    ½ cup butter or margarine
    1 teaspoon grated lemon peel
    4 eggs
    1½ cups California raisins (mixed golden and regular)
    ⅓ cup pine nuts or slivered almonds (reserve 1
        tablespoon)
    1 cup mixed chopped candied fruits
    Powdered sugar

In large mixer bowl, mix yeast, sugar, salt and 2 cups of the flour. Heat water with butter and lemon peel over low heat until very warm (120-130 degrees). Add liquids to dry ingredients. Beat for 2 minutes at medium speed. Add 2 cups more of the flour, and the eggs; beat 3 minutes. Stir in almost all of remaining flour. Knead dough on floured board about 8 minutes, until smooth and elastic. Place in buttered bowl. Cover and let rise in warm place until doubled in bulk—about 2 hours. Punch down; knead in raisins, nuts and fruit. Shape into 2 round loaves. Place on greased baking sheets; brush lightly with butter. Let rise 1 to 1½ hours until doubled. With sharp knife, slash top of each loaf to make a cross. Bake at 350 degrees for 45 to 55 minutes. Turn onto rack. Brush lightly with butter. Garnish with reserved nuts. Dust with powdered sugar. Serve with Orange Butter (recipe follows). Extra loaves freeze well.   *Yield: 2 loaves*

Orange Butter

    1 stick butter or margarine
    1½ cups powdered sugar
    2 tablespoons orange juice
    1 tablespoon grated orange peel

Mix all ingredients; beat until fluffy. Serve as spread for panettone.   *Yield: 1 cup*

Favorite recipe from **California Raisin Advisory Board**

Sparkling Amaretto & Cognac

    1½ oz. HIRAM WALKER Amaretto & Cognac
    Soda

Pack a highball glass with ice. Pour in Amaretto & Cognac. Fill with soda and garnish with lime wedge.

Amaretto Strawberries

    2 oz. HIRAM WALKER Amaretto
    1 pint fresh strawberries
    Vanilla ice cream

Marinate strawberries overnight in Amaretto. Serve over ice cream, sprinkled with slivered almonds.   *Serves 4*

Lemon Ice

    1½ cups water
    1 cup sugar
    ½ cup BERTOLLI® Soave Classico Wine
    Grated rind of 4 lemons
    ¾ to 1 cup lemon juice

Heat water and sugar to boiling in saucepan; boil 3 minutes. Cool. Mix all ingredients. Freeze in 9-inch pan until firm, about 3 hours.   *8 servings*

Ditalini Dessert

    1 cup GIOIA® Ditalini
    1 cup crushed pineapple, drained thoroughly
    1 cup miniature marshmallows
    1 can sweetened condensed milk
    2 tablespoons fresh lemon juice
    ¼ cup maraschino cherries, chopped
    2 cups graham cracker crumbs
    ½ cup melted margarine

Cook the **GIOIA® Ditalini** in 2 quarts of boiling, salted water for 12-14 minutes. Drain and rinse with cold water, set aside.

Mix the graham cracker crumbs with the melted margarine. Save ½ cup of the crumb mixture. Press the rest in the bottom of an 8 inch square pan. Mix the cooked Ditalini with the pineapple, marshmallows, cherries, sweetened condensed milk and lemon juice. Pour over crust. Sprinkle remaining crumbs on top. Chill for 3 hours. Cut into small squares and serve.

Strawberries Cardinal

    3 cups strawberries
    One 10 oz. pkg. frozen raspberries
    ⅓ cup confectioners sugar
    ¼ cup CHAMBORD
    1 cup sweetened whipped cream

Wash and hull strawberries. Divide among four long stemmed glasses. Puree raspberries in a blender with sugar and **CHAMBORD**. Strain to remove seeds. Pour over strawberries and chill six hours. Dollop whipped cream over berries before serving.

Napoli Fruit Shake

Combine in blender container:
    2 cups DEL MONTE Pineapple-Grapefruit Juice
        Drink
    1 can (8 oz.) DEL MONTE Fruit Cocktail
    2 cups vanilla ice cream

Cover and blend until smooth. Garnish with nutmeg.

Angostura® Zabaglione

4 egg yolks
½ cup sugar
2 tablespoons orange juice
2 teaspoons grated orange rind
1½ teaspoons ANGOSTURA® Aromatic Bitters
4 egg whites

In the top part of a double boiler beat egg yolks with ¼ cup of the sugar over hot not boiling water until thick and lemon colored. Slowly beat in orange juice, rind and ANGOSTURA®. Continue beating until mixture is very thick and holds peaks. Beat egg whites until stiff and gradually beat in remaining sugar 1 table-spoon at a time until stiff and glossy. Fold egg whites into egg yolk mixture. Serve warm in dessert glasses or spooned over fruit.

Yield: 6-8 servings

Lemon Snow with Nesselro Sauce

1 envelope unflavored gelatin
½ cup sugar
¼ teaspoon salt
1¼ cups hot water
1 (6 ounce) can frozen lemonade, unthawed
2 egg whites
RAFFETTO® Nesselro

Combine gelatin, sugar and salt in a small bowl. Add hot water and stir until gelatin is dissolved. Add lemonade and blend well. Chill mixture in refrigerator until slightly thickened. Place bowl in another bowl of ice and water. Add unbeaten egg whites. Beat until mixture forms soft peaks. Pour into a 1½ quart ring mold or other mold. Chill in refrigerator until firm. Unmold on a chilled serving plate and serve with Nesselro sauce. *8 servings*

Cannoli con Frutta

3¼ cups all-purpose flour
2 tablespoons granulated sugar
½ teaspoon salt
4 tablespoons softened butter or margarine
1 tablespoon grated lemon rind
2 eggs
½ cup white wine vinegar
1 egg white
Vegetable oil

Filling:
1 can (30-ounce) fruit cocktail
½ pint heavy cream, whipped
½ pint ricotta cheese
½ teaspoon lemon juice
½ teaspoon grated lemon rind
½ teaspoon rum extract
¼ cup confectioner's sugar

Combine flour, sugar and salt in medium size bowl. Cut in butter until mixture resembles coarse crumbs. Stir in lemon rind, eggs and vinegar. Mix with fork until consistency of pie pastry. If too dry add more vinegar, a few drops at a time. Roll dough between hands into a ball. Let rest 15 minutes. Divide dough into quarters. Roll each on lightly floured board, as thin as possible. Cut dough into 4½-inch circles. Wrap each circle around cannoli form, seal-ing edges well with egg white. If no cannoli forms are available,

make forms cut out of aluminum foil. Heat oil (2 inches) to 400 degrees F. Fry dough around forms until golden brown, about 2 minutes. Drain on paper towels. Remove cannoli forms after shells have slightly cooled.

FILLING:
Drain fruit cocktail. Combine filling of whipped cream, ricotta cheese, lemon juice, lemon rind and rum extract. Fold in fruit cocktail. Fill shells with filling. Dust with confectioner's sugar just before serving. Can be prepared ahead and frozen until ready to serve. *Yield: approximately 1½ dozen*

Favorite recipe from **Cling Peach Advisory Board**

Glazed Strawberry Pear Pie

1⅓ cups unsifted flour
⅓ cup ground PLANTERS® Almonds
1 tablespoon sugar
6 tablespoons butter
3 to 4 tablespoons cold water
1½ cups water
⅓ cup sugar
½ cup AMARETTO DI AMORE® Liqueur
4 pears, peeled, halved and cored
1½ teaspoons unflavored gelatin
8 to 10 medium strawberries, sliced

Combine flour, **PLANTERS® Almonds** and sugar; cut in butter until mixture resembles coarse meal. Stir in enough cold water to shape pastry into a ball. Roll pastry out between two sheets of wax paper to a 12-inch circle. Fit into a 10-inch quiche pan. Prick bottom slightly. Bake at 375°F. for 10 to 12 minutes, or until golden. Cool.

In a large skillet combine water, sugar and ¼ cup **AMARETTO DI AMORE® Liqueur.** Place pears cut side down in skillet. Cover and simmer over low heat 25 to 30 minutes, or until pears are tender. Remove pears and drain well on paper towels; chill. Reserve ¾ cup poaching liquid.

Soften gelatin in ¼ cup **AMARETTO DI AMORE® Liqueur.** Stir in reserved hot poaching liquid. Chill slightly until syrupy. Spoon a thin layer of gelatin glaze on the bottom of prepared crust. Arrange pears, cut side down, in prepared crust with sliced straw-berries in the center and around the edges. Spoon remaining glaze over fruit to coat. Chill until firm. Serve with whipped cream if desired. *Makes 8 servings*

Frozen Macaroon Pie

1 (9-inch) baked pastry shell, cooled or graham cracker crumb crust
1 pint orange sherbet, softened
1 cup (½ pint) whipping cream
½ cup firmly-packed COLONIAL® Light Golden Brown Sugar
1 cup coarsely crushed crisp macaroon cookies
¾ cup toasted coconut
½ cup chopped toasted almonds

Spread sherbet in bottom of pastry shell. Freeze while preparing topping. In small mixer bowl, beat cream, slowly adding sugar, until stiff; fold in cookies, ½ cup coconut and the almonds. Spread on top of sherbet; garnish with remaining coconut. Freeze until firm.

Makes one 9-inch pie

Ricotta Pie
(Torta di Ricotta)

2 cups flour
1 teaspoon baking powder
¼ teaspoon salt
¾ cup butter or margarine
3 tablespoons brandy
1½ pounds (3 cups) ricotta
1 tablespoon flour
1 cup **DOMINO® Granulated Sugar**
¼ teaspoon salt
4 eggs slightly beaten
2 tablespoons finely chopped citron
3 tablespoons chopped toasted almonds
½ cup mini semi-sweet chocolate chips or 3 oz. grated
  semi-sweet chocolate
1½ teaspoons vanilla
DOMINO® Confectioners 10X Sugar

Sift together flour, baking powder, and ¼ teaspoon salt. Cut in butter until fine. Stir in brandy until dough sticks together. Wrap in wax paper and chill 30 minutes. Roll ⅔ of dough between floured wax paper. Peel off top sheet of wax paper. Turn dough over a 10-inch pie plate. Gently peel off paper. Fit dough into pan, allowing ½-inch overhang. (Pastry is easy to repair with scraps of dough if it tears.)

Combine ricotta, 1 tablespoon flour, sugar, and ¼ teaspoon salt. Stir in eggs. Add citron, almonds, chocolate, and vanilla. Roll remaining pastry between floured wax paper. Peel off top paper, cut pastry into strips. Pour cheese filling into crust. Arrange pastry strips on top; fold edge of bottom crust over ends of strips, press together and flute. Bake at 375°F for 40 to 45 minutes until pie puffs across top and is done. Cool. Refrigerate pie. Serve with confectioners sugar sprinkled over the top.

Makes 8 to 10 servings

KNOX.

Cappuccino Cheesecake

1 envelope **KNOX® Unflavored Gelatine**
⅓ cup sugar
¾ cup boiling water
1 cup (8 oz.) sour cream
1 package (8 oz.) cream cheese, softened
⅓ cup coffee liqueur
1 teaspoon vanilla extract
½ cup chopped pecans or walnuts
Zwieback Crumb Crust*

In large bowl, mix unflavored gelatine with sugar; add boiling water and stir until gelatine is completely dissolved. With electric mixer, add sour cream, cream cheese, liqueur and vanilla, one at a time, beating well after each addition. Fold in nuts. Turn into prepared crust; chill until firm.   *Makes about 8 servings*

*Zwieback Crumb Crust

In small bowl, combine 1 cup zwieback cracker crumbs, 2 tablespoons sugar and 3 tablespoons melted butter or margarine. Press into 9-inch pie pan; chill.

Apricot Choco-Nilla Cheesecake

1 cup graham cracker crumbs
3 tablespoons butter or margarine
2 tablespoons sugar
¼ teaspoon cinnamon
2 pounds farmer cheese
4 eggs
⅓ cup milk
1 teaspoon vanilla
1¼ cups sugar
¼ cup flour
2 squares (2 ounces) semisweet chocolate, melted
2 cans (17 ounces each) apricot halves, drained
2 tablespoons water
2 tablespoons cornstarch

Thoroughly blend together graham cracker crumbs, butter, 2 tablespoons sugar and cinnamon. Firmly press into an even layer on bottom of lightly-oiled 8 inch spring form pan. In large electric mixer bowl, beat cheese until smooth. Beat in eggs one at a time; stir in milk and vanilla. Mix in 1¼ cups sugar and flour until smooth. Stir melted chocolate into half of cheese mixture; pour into pan. Carefully pour vanilla layer on top of first layer. Bake in 350°F. oven 1 hour and 15 minutes or until toothpick inserted in center comes out clean. Turn off oven and open door; let cake remain in oven 30 minutes. Cool on wire cake rack. Puree 1 can drained apricots in electric blender. In small saucepan, stir together water and cornstarch until smooth; mix in pureed apricots. Cook and stir until mixture boils and thickens. Remove from heat, cool slightly. Spread on top of cheesecake; top with remaining apricots. Chill in refrigerator until cold.

Makes 16 servings

Note: Using farmer cheese instead of cream cheese reduces calories in cake by about 2180.

Favorite recipe from **California Apricot Advisory Board**

Low Cal Cheesecake

1 cup graham cracker crumbs
¾ cup sugar, divided
¼ cup butter or margarine, softened
1 container (15 ounces) small curd cottage cheese
4 eggs
½ cup evaporated skim milk
3 Tablespoons lemon or orange juice
1 teaspoon lemon or orange peel
¼ teaspoon salt
¼ cup flour
1 package (10 ounces) **Frozen STOKELY'S® Red
  Raspberries, in Syrup,** thawed

Preheat oven to 300° F. Grease lightly a spring-form pan. Mix cracker crumbs, ¼ cup sugar and butter. Press into bottom of prepared pan. In blender mix until smooth cheese, eggs, milk, remaining sugar, lemon juice, lemon peel, and salt. Add flour and blend a few seconds. Pour over cracker crumbs. Bake 1 hour or until firm. Cool completely before removing side of pan. Pour raspberries over cheesecake and serve at once.

Makes 14 servings

Note: Canned fruit may be substituted for raspberries.

Acknowledgments

The Editors of CONSUMER GUIDE® wish to thank the companies and organizations listed for use of their recipes and artwork. For further information contact the following:

A.1.—Heublein Inc.
Grocery Products Group
Farmington, CT 06032

Ac´cent International, Inc.
Pet Incorporated
400 S. Fourth St.
St. Louis, MO 63166

Almadén Vineyards
P.O. Box 5010
San Jose, CA 95150

Amaretto Di Amore®, see Wile, Julius,
Sons & Co.

Amaretto Di Saronno®—Foreign Vintages, Inc.
95 Madison Avenue
New York, NY 10016

Amaretto from Galliano®, *see* "21"
Brands, Inc.

American Beauty®, *see* Pillsbury Company

American Dry Milk Institute, Inc.
130 N. Franklin St.
Chicago, IL 60606

American Egg Board
1460 Renaissance Dr.
Park Ridge, IL 60068

American Home Foods
685 Third Ave.
New York, NY 10017

American Soybean Association
P.O. Box 27300
St. Louis, MO 63141

Angostura International Ltd.
Rahway, NJ 07065

Apple Growers of Washington State, The
Pacific Kitchens
300 Elliott Avenue West
Seattle, WA 98119

Armanino Farms of California
1945 Carroll Ave.
San Francisco, CA 94124

Atalanta Corp.
17 Varick St.
New York, NY 10013

Aunt Nellie's Foods Inc.
Clyman, WI 53016

B&B, see Wile, Julius, Sons & Co.

*Bac*Os®, *see* General Mills, Inc.

Baltimore Spice Company, The
P.O. Box 5858
Baltimore, MD 21208

Banquet Foods Corp.
Ballwin, MO 63011

Bertolli U.S.A.
P.O. Box 931
So. San Francisco, CA 94080

Best Foods
Englewood Cliffs, NJ 07632

Betty Crocker®, *see* General Mills, Inc.

BinB®—Clorox Company
P.O. Box 24305
Oakland, CA 94623

Birds Eye®—General Foods
White Plains, NY 10625

Bisquick®, *see* General Mills, Inc.

Blue Diamond®—California Almond
Growers Exchange
P.O. Box 1768
Sacramento, CA 95808

Bob Evans Farm
P.O. Box 07863
Columbus, OH 43207

Booth Fisheries Corp.
2 North Riverside Plaza
Chicago, IL 60606

Borden Inc.
180 E. Broad St.
Columbus, OH 43215

Bridgford Foods Corp.
1308 N. Patt St.
Anaheim, CA 92801

Brilliant Seafood, Inc.
315 Northern Ave.
Boston, MA 02210

Brown's Best—Kelley Bean Co.
Morrill, NE 69358

Brownberry
Oconomowoc, WI 53066

Buddig, Carl, & Company
11914 S. Peoria St.
Chicago, IL 60643

Budweiser®—Anheuser-Busch, Inc.
St. Louis, MO 63118

Buitoni Foods Corp.
450 Huyler St.
South Hackensack, NJ 07606

Bumble Bee®, *see* Castle & Cooke Foods

Butter Buds®, *see* Cumberland Packing Corp.

Butterball® *Swift's Premium*®, *see* Swift & Co.

California Apricot Advisory Board
1280 Boulevard Way
Walnut Creek, CA 94595

California Brandy Advisory Board
426 Pacific Avenue
San Francisco, CA 94133

California Iceberg Lettuce Commission
P.O. Box 3354
Monterey, CA 93940

California Raisin Advisory Board
P.O. Box 5335
Fresno, CA 93726

Campbell Soup Co.
Camden, NJ 08101

Castle & Cooke Foods
P.O. Box 3928
San Francisco, CA 94119

Chambord—Charles Jacquin et Cie., Inc.
2633 Trenton Ave.
Philadelphia, PA 19125

Cheez-It®, *see* Sunshine Biscuits, Inc.

Cheez-Ola®, *see* Fisher Cheese Co.

Chef Boy-Ar-Dee®, *see* American Home Foods

Chicken of the Sea®—Ralston Purina Co.
St. Louis, MO 63188

Claussen, see Oscar Mayer Foods Corp.

Clear Springs Trout Co., Inc.
Buhl, ID 83316

Cling Peach Advisory Board
One California St.
San Francisco, CA 94111

Coca-Cola Company, The
P.O. Drawer 1734
Atlanta, GA 30303

Colonial Sugars, Inc.
P.O. Box 1646
Mobile, AL 36633

Consolidated Dairy Products Co.
Box C 19099
Seattle, WA 98109

Contadina Foods, Inc.
Sub. of Carnation Company
5045 Wilshire Blvd.
Los Angeles, CA 90036

Cookin' Good™—Showell Farms
Showell, MD 21862

Country Pride Foods Ltd.
El Dorado, AR 71730

County Line Cheese Company
Auburn, IN 46706

Creamette Co., The
428 North First St.
Minneapolis, MN 55401

Crisco®, *see* Procter & Gamble Company

Cumberland Packing Corp.
2 Cumberland Street
Brooklyn, NY 11205

Dannon Company, Inc., The
22-11 38th Ave.
Long Island City, NY 11101

Dari-Lite, see Consolidated Dairy Products Co.

Darigold, see Consolidated Dairy Products Co.

Del Monte Corporation
P.O. Box 3575
San Francisco, CA 94105

Delft Blue-Provimi Inc.
Watertown, WI 53094

Dole®, *see* Castle & Cooke Foods

Domino®—Amstar Corporation
1251 Avenue of the Americas
New York, NY 10020

Dore Rice Mill, The
Crowley, LA 70526

Dorman, N., & Co.
Syosset, NY 11791

Dromedary, see Nabisco Brands, Inc.

Dubonnet—Schenley Affiliated Brands Corp.
888 Seventh Avenue
New York, NY 10106

Durkee Foods
Strongsville, OH 44136

Eagle® *Brand, see* Borden Inc.

Elam Mills
2625 Gardner Road
Broadview, IL 60153

Enrico's—Ventre Packing Co., Inc.
373 Spencer
Syracuse, NY 13204

Estee Corp., The
Parsippany, NJ 07054

Falbo, S., Cheese Co., Inc.
1931 N. 15th Ave.
Melrose Park, IL 60160

Featherweight®—Chicago Dietetic Supply, Inc.
405 E. Shawmut Ave.
La Grange, IL 60525

Filippo Berio—Berio Importing Corp.
P.O. Box 239
Scarsdale, NY 10583

Finlandia Cheese, *see* Atalanta Corp.

Fisher Boy®—Consumers Fish Co.
2 North Riverside Plaza
Chicago, IL 60606

Fisher Cheese Co.
Wapakoneta, OH 45895

Florida Department of Natural Resources
3900 Commonwealth Blvd.
Tallahassee, FL 32303

Foulds Inc.
520 E. Church St.
Libertyville, IL 60048

French, R. T., Co.
Rochester, NY 14609

Frigo Cheese Corp.
Lena, WI 54139

Frito-Lay, Inc.
P.O. Box 35034
Dallas, TX 75235

Furman Canning Co.
Northumberland, PA 17857

Furmano's®, *see* Furman Canning Co.

G. Washington's®, *see* American
Home Foods

Gallo Salame
250 Brannan St.
San Francisco, CA 94107

Geisha® *Brand*—Nozaki America, Inc.
1 World Trade Center
New York, NY 10048

General Mills, Inc.
Minneapolis, MN 55440

Gioia Macaroni Co. Inc.
P.O. Box 237
Buffalo, NY 14240

Gold Pure Food Products
895 McDonald Ave.
Brooklyn, NY 11218

Golden Grain Macaroni Co.
San Leandro, CA 94578

Goodman, A., & Sons, Inc.
325 Marcus Blvd.
Deer Park, NY 11729

Goya Foods Corp.
100 Sea View Dr.
Secaucus, NJ 07094

Green Giant®, *see* Pillsbury Company

Gulf and South Atlantic Fisheries
Development Foundation
5401 W. Kennedy Blvd.
Tampa, FL 33609

Hamburger Helper®, *see* General Mills, Inc.

Harvest Brand®, *see* National Oats Company

Health Valley Natural Foods
700 Union Street
Montebello, CA 90640

Heinz U.S.A.
P.O. Box 57
Pittsburgh, PA 15230

Hellmann's®, *see* Best Foods

Henri's Food Products Co. Inc.
2730 W. Silver Spring Dr.
Milwaukee, WI 53209

Hershey Foods Corp.
Hershey, PA 17033

Hi Ho Crackers®, *see* Sunshine Biscuits, Inc.

High Liner®—National Sea Products Ltd.
555 Burnham Thorpe Rd.
Etobicoke, Ontario, Canada M9C 2Y3

Hillshire Farm®, *see* Kahn's and Co.

Hiram Walker & Sons, Inc.
P.O. Box 33006
Detroit, MI 48232

Holland House Brands Co.
Ridgefield, NJ 07657

Holmes, *see* Port Clyde Foods, Inc.

Hormel, Geo. A., & Co.
Austin, MN 55912

Hunt-Wesson Kitchens
Fullerton, CA 92634

Ideal Macaroni Co.
Bedford Heights, OH 44146

Jeno's
525 Lake Avenue South
Duluth, MN 55802

Jimmy Dean Meat Company, Inc.
1341 W. Mockingbird Ln.
Dallas, TX 75247

Kahn's and Company
3241 Spring Grove Ave.
Cincinnati, OH 45225

Keebler Company
Elmhurst, IL 60126

Kellogg Company
Battle Creek, MI 49016

King Arthur—Sands, Taylor & Wood Co.
155 N. Beacon St.
Brighton, MA 02135

Knox®, *see* Lipton, Thomas J., Inc.

Kretschmer—International Multifoods
Box 2942
Minneapolis, MN 55402

La Rosa, V., & Sons, Inc.
Warminster, PA 18974

La Sauce®—Armour and Company
Phoenix, AZ 85077

Land O'Lakes, Inc.
Arden Hills, MN 55440

Lawry's Foods, Inc.
570 West Avenue 26
Los Angeles, CA 90065

Lea & Perrins, Inc.
Fair Lawn, NJ 07410

Leafy Greens Council
503 S. Oak Park Avenue
Oak Park, IL 60304

Libby, McNeill & Libby, Inc.
200 S. Michigan Ave.
Chicago, IL 60604

Lindsay International Inc.
Visalia, CA 93277

Lipton, Thomas J., Inc.
Englewood Cliffs, NJ 07632

Liquore Galliano®, see "21" Brands, Inc.

Louis Rich Company
Div. Oscar Mayer Foods Corp.
Madison, WI 53707

Malt-O-Meal Co.
1520 TCF Tower
Minneapolis, MN 55402

Martha White Foods Inc.
P.O. Box 58
Nashville, TN 37202

Mazola®, see Best Foods

Merkt Cheese Co., Inc.
Bristol, WI 53104

Michigan Bean Commission
P.O. Box 22037
Lansing, MI 48909

Minute Maid®—The Coca-Cola Company
Foods Division
P.O. Box 2079
Houston, TX 77001

Morton Salt
110 N. Wacker Dr.
Chicago, IL 60606

Mu Tofu Shop
1735 W. Greenleaf
Chicago, IL 60626

Mueller, C. F., Company
180 Baldwin Avenue
Jersey City, NJ 07306

Nabisco Brands, Inc.
625 Madison Avenue
New York, NY 10022

Nalley's Fine Foods
3303 S. 35th
Tacoma, WA 98411

National Hot Dog & Sausage Council
400 W. Madison
Chicago, IL 60606

National Live Stock & Meat Board
Pork Industry Group
444 N. Michigan Avenue
Chicago, IL 60611

National Marine Fisheries Service
3300 Whitehaven, N.W.
Washington, DC 20235

National Oats Company Inc.
1515 H Avenue NE
Cedar Rapids, IA 52402

North American Blueberry Council
Marmora, NJ 08223

Ore-Ida Foods, Inc.
P.O. Box 10
Boise, ID 83707

Oscar Mayer Foods Corp.
Madison, WI 53707

P&R, see San Giorgio-Skinner, Inc.

Pacific Pearl Seafoods
Bellevue, WA 98004

Pastorelli Food Products Inc.
164 N. Sangamon St.
Chicago, IL 60607

Pepperidge Farm, Inc.
Norwalk, CT 06856

Perdue Farms Inc.
Salisbury, MD 21801

Pernod®—Austin Nichols & Co. Inc.
1290 Avenue of the Americas
New York, NY 10104

Pillsbury Company, The
608 2nd Avenue South
Minneapolis, MN 55402

Pizza-Mate®, see Fisher Cheese Co.

Polly-O®—Pollio Dairy Products Corp.
Port Washington, NY 11050

Port Clyde Foods, Inc.
Falmouth, ME 04105

Precious®—California Cheese Company
P.O. Box 3196 Station D
San Jose, CA 95116

Procter & Gamble Company, The
Cincinnati, OH 45202

Puritan®, see Procter & Gamble Company

R·F®, see Ravarino & Freschi, Inc.

Raffetto®—Iroquois Grocery Products, Inc.
111 High Ridge Road
Stamford, CT 06905

Ragu®—Chesebrough-Pond's Inc.
Trumbull, CT 06611

Rath Packing Company, The
Waterloo, IA 50704

Ravarino & Freschi, Inc.
4651 Shaw Blvd.
St. Louis, MO 63100

ReaLemon®, see Borden Inc.

Red Cross®, see Ravarino & Freschi, Inc.

Red Star®, see Universal Foods Corp.

Redpack—California Canners and Growers
3100 Ferry Building
San Francisco, CA 94106

Rhodes™—Dakota Bake-N-Serv, Inc.
Jamestown, ND 58401-0688

Rice-A-Roni®, see Golden Grain Macaroni Co.

Ritz, see Nabisco Brands, Inc.

Rokeach, I., & Sons, Inc.
560 Sylvan Ave.
Englewood Cliffs, NJ 07632

Roman Meal Co.
P.O. Box 11126
Tacoma, WA 98411

Ronzoni Macaroni Co., Inc.
50-02 Northern Blvd.
Long Island City, NY 11101

S&W Fine Foods, Inc.
San Mateo, CA 94402

Sambuca from Galliano®, see "21" Brands, Inc.

San Giorgio-Skinner, Inc.
One Chocolate Avenue
Hershey, PA 17033

Sanwa Foods Inc.
530 Baldwin Park
City of Industry, CA 91746

Sara Lee, Kitchens of
Deerfield, IL 60015

Sargento Cheese Company Inc.
Plymouth, WI 53073

Sealtest®—Kraft Inc.-Dairy Group
P.O. Box 7830
Philadelphia, PA 19101

Shoal Lake Wild Rice Ltd.
P.O. Box 577
Keewatin, Ontario, Canada POX 1CO

Sizzlean®, see Swift & Company

Snack Mate, see Nabisco Brands, Inc.

South African Rock Lobster Service Corp.
450 Seventh Ave.
New York, NY 10123

Spam®, see Hormel, Geo. A., & Co.

Stella®, see Universal Foods Corp.

Stokely-Van Camp, Inc.
941 N. Meridian St.
Indianapolis, IN 46206

Success®—Riviana Foods Inc.
P.O. Box 2636
Houston, TX 77001

Sunkist Growers, Inc.
Van Nuys, CA 91409

Sunshine Biscuits, Inc.
245 Park Avenue
New York, NY 10017

Sweet 'N Low®, see Cumberland
Packing Corp.

Sweetlite™—Batterlite Whitlock Inc.
P.O. Box 259
Springfield, IL 62705-0259

Swift & Company
Oak Brook, IL 60521

Tabasco®—McIlhenny Co.
Avery Island, LA 70513

3-Minute Brand®, see National Oats Company

Tia Maria®—W. A. Taylor & Co.
825 South Bayshore Dr.
Miami, FL 33131

Top Ramen®—Nissin Foods (USA) Co., Inc.
2001 W. Rosecrans Avenue
Gardena, CA 90249

"21" Brands, Inc.
75 Rockefeller Plaza
New York, NY 10019

Tyson Foods, Inc.
Springdale, AR 72764

Uncle Ben's Foods
P.O. Box 1752
Houston, TX 77001

United Fresh Fruit & Vegetable Association
North Washington at Madison
Alexandria, VA 22314

Universal Foods Corporation
433 E. Michigan
Milwaukee, WI 53201

Van De Kamp's Frozen Foods
Santa Fe Springs, CA 90670

Veg-All®—The Larsen Company
P.O. Box 1127
Green Bay, WI 54305

Villa Antinori, see Wile, Julius, Sons & Co.

Wakefield Seafoods Corp.
Bellevue, WA 98004

Weaver, Victor F., Inc.
New Holland, PA 17557

Welch Foods Inc.
Westfield, NY 14787

Wesson®, see Hunt-Wesson Kitchens

Wile, Julius, Sons & Co., Inc.
Lake Success, NY 11042

Wish-Bone®, see Lipton, Thomas J., Inc.

Witt, F. W., & Company, Inc.
Yorkville, IL 60560

Wyler's®, see Borden Inc.

Index